A Student's Guide
to Camus

STUDENTS' GUIDES
TO EUROPEAN LITERATURE

General Editor: Brian Masters

Molière, by Brian Masters
Sartre, by Brian Masters
Goethe, by F. J. Lamport
Rabelais, by Brian Masters
Corneille, by J. H. Broome
Böll, by Enid Macpherson
Kafka, by Anthony Thorlby
Saint-Exupéry, by Brian Masters
Racine, by Philip Butler
Camus, by Brian Masters

A Student's Guide to Camus

by
BRIAN MASTERS

HEINEMANN EDUCATIONAL
BOOKS · LONDON

Heinemann Educational Books Ltd
LONDON EDINBURGH MELBOURNE AUCKLAND TORONTO
HONG KONG SINGAPORE KUALA LUMPUR
IBADAN NAIROBI JOHANNESBURG
NEW DELHI

ISBN 0 435 37584 9

© Brian Masters 1974
First published 1974

Published by
Heinemann Educational Books Ltd
48 Charles Street, London W1X 8AH
Printed in Great Britain by
Richard Clay (The Chaucer Press) Ltd
Bungay, Suffolk

Contents

Foreword		vii
Acknowledgements		ix
Chapter One :	BEFORE *L'ETRANGER*	1
	Early Life	1
	Character	9
	First Writing	11
Chapter Two :	*L'ETRANGER*	19
Chapter Three :	*LE MYTHE DE SISYPHE*	35
	Le Malentendu and *Caligula*	54
Chapter Four :	*LA PESTE*	60
	The Characters	64
	Moral	82
	Les Justes	93
Chapter Five :	*L'HOMME REVOLTE*	98
	The Quarrel with Sartre	106
	Politics and Journalism	110
Chapter Six :	*LA CHUTE*	117
Bibliography		129

To Gerry and Phyl

Foreword

This book is intended for the use of students and for the general reader. For the sake of the former, I have used the most widely available editions of Camus's works when quoting, and the page references apply, where possible, to educational editions. A complete list of the editions I have used is to be found in the bibliography. For the general reader, the quotations are translated in footnote. For the most part, these translations are taken from already published sources, for which the list is also included in the bibliography. Occasionally, however, an alternative translation is offered, and my own translations have had to be used where no other exists. In such cases, the reader will find BM in brackets after the quotation.

Acknowledgements

I should like to record my indebtedness to the Librairie Galli-mard for their kind permission to quote from the works of Albert Camus, of which they control the copyright. I am similarly grateful to Messrs Hamish Hamilton for allowing me to quote from translations published by them (*The Outsider*, *The Myth of Sisyphus*, *The Plague*, *The Rebel*, *The Fall*, *Lyrical and Critical*, *Resistance*, *Rebellion and Death*), and to Messrs Alfred A. Knopf Inc., for permission to quote from their translation of *Les Justes* (in *Caligula and Three Other Plays*).

This study could not have been written without the generous hospitality of Lord and Lady Londonderry, to whom I wish to express my gratitude. I am also indebted to Mrs D. P. Sherwood for her efficient typing of the manuscript, and to Mr Brian Staveley for his careful reading and helpful suggestions.

B.M.

Wynyard, 1973

1

Before *L'Etranger*

Early Life

The reputation of Albert Camus as the Philosopher of the Absurd appears to be indestructible. Yet he was not a philosopher, nor did he have patience with abstract concepts. He confessed himself embarrassed, even irritated, by the label, conferred upon him by over-zealous literary commentators. Certainly he wrote about the painful absurdity of human life, but he was by no means the first to do so, nor was this the only theme of his work. He never intended that it should be more than a starting-point.[1] Writing in 1950, eight years after the publication of *L'Etranger* and *Le Mythe de Sisyphe*, when his influence over the young was enormous, and he was already well on the way towards a kind of canonization, he objected to the notion that his was a literature of despair. Is it not possible, he said, to write an essay on the Absurd without being labelled a Prophet of the Absurd? After all, one might write about incest, without for all that leaping upon one's unfortunate sister. All his life, Camus was at pains to reject the attribution of pessimism to his writing. Far from being pessimistic, his whole work postulates an alternative to the nihilism which was fashionable when he grew up, and which the horrifying experience of the war made almost inescapable. The real pessimism, says Camus, lies not in acknowledging the injustice, cruelty and absurdity which govern the world, but in giving one's assent to them. This he resolutely refused to do:

[1] See *L'Homme Révolté*, p. 19.

> Mais le vrai pessimisme, qui se rencontre, consiste à
> renchérir sur tant de cruauté et d'infamie. Je n'ai jamais
> cessé, pour ma part, de lutter contre ce déshonneur et
> je ne hais que les cruels.[1]

This is the central idea which pervades all of Camus's work.
He strove always to assert the dignity and respect due to man in
spite of the indignities inflicted upon him in the name of
abstract concepts. The path he trod was a difficult one. It
consisted in rescuing some worth from a valueless world. He
was not blind to the tragic nature of man's fate, but unlike
many of his contemporaries he would not admit that lucidity
should lead inevitably to despair. In a world where values are
relative, he saw no need to negate them all, or to seek refuge in a
mystical consolation. He would not accept any but human
standards of judgement, would refuse any value which did
not respect the individual, yet he managed to extract from this
austerity a cause for rejoicing, not an excuse for despondency.
The world may be unjust, he said, yet there is a human quality
of justice which can, and should, be cherished. The world may
be cruel, but cruelty can be alleviated by the human quality of
mercy. The world may be absurd, but man is not:

> Je continue à croire que ce monde n'a pas de sens
> supérieur. Mais je sais que quelque chose en lui a du sens
> et c'est l'homme, parce qu'il est le seul être à exiger d'en
> avoir.[2]

These are not the conclusions of a philosophic mind, but
rather the emotional responses of a deeply sensitive man.
Camus was not a professional intellectual. He was an ordinary
man who spoke for ordinary people, but he had the gift of
vivid and persuasive expression. He did not indulge in metaphysical speculation. My philosophy, he wrote in his notebook,

---

[1] *Eté*, p. 149. 'But real pessimism, which does exist, lies in going one
better than all this cruelty and shame. For my part, I have never ceased
fighting against this dishonour, and I hate only the cruel.'

[2] *Lettres à un Ami Allemand*, p. 74. 'I continue to believe that this world
has no ultimate meaning. But I know that something in it has meaning,
and that is man, because he is the only creature to insist on having one.'

is that a quarter of an hour after my death I shall no longer be alive. There is no contempt in this dismissal of metaphysical preoccupations, merely a statement of priorities. Camus was concerned with life and death, with people that live and die, not with philosophy. Consequently, the opinions which he offers (and he never claims that they are more than opinions) are the expression of truths which he feels passionately and intuitively, though their logical sequence may not stand up to the scrutiny of academic philosophers. They do not find their origin in cerebral gymnastics, but in painful experience, and in sympathetic observation. Hence, when Camus talks about the Absurd, he is articulating an emotion felt by all, he is not proposing a school of thought. 'Je ne suis pas un philosophe', he writes, 'et je ne sais parler que de ce que j'ai vécu.'[1]

Camus maintained that an examination of his life was not strictly relevant to an understanding of his work. He did not care for the biographical approach to critical analysis. But if, as he says, his views are rooted in personal experience, it is as well to discover something of that experience.

Camus was born into total poverty. Among writers to have achieved international status, he is one of the comparatively few who emerged from the humblest of the working-class poor. His parents lived in Mondovi, in Algeria, where Albert Camus was born on 7 November 1913. His father, barely literate, and of Alsatian stock, was an agricultural worker on a vineyard. His mother, *née* Catherine Sintès, was of Spanish origin, and was also illiterate. There was one older brother, Lucien, and a deeply Catholic grandmother.

Eight months after Camus was born, his father was mobilized. The family were never to see him again, for he was killed at the first Battle of the Marne in September 1914. Although Camus never knew him, he felt keenly, in later years, the injustice of his stupid death and the additional suffering which it heaped upon his mother.

Catherine Camus, a widow at twenty-five years, then left

[1] *Actuelles* I, p. 83. 'I am not a philosopher and can only talk about experiences I have lived through.' (BM)

Mondovi for Algiers. Here she found a two-room flat in the poorest section, Belcourt, and established her family of two small sons, grandmother, and semi-paralysed uncle. She took work as a charwoman to feed the family. Food was not always plentiful. The atmosphere in that flat, with an overbearing old grandmother, short-tempered and religious, a sick uncle, and a broken widow, given to long silences, must have been claustrophobic. Outside, life was not much more cheerful. Camus recalls having seen children in rags fighting over food in dustbins, with dogs joining in the scramble.[1] Experiences such as these had a greater influence upon him than his later reading of Marx, as he was one day to admit.

At the age of five, Camus went to the local primary school in the rue Aumerat. He was soon noticed by the modest but prescient teacher Louis Germain, who was aware that Camus was brighter than most, and gave him extra lessons out of school hours. Germain persuaded Madame Camus to let her son sit the examinations for a scholarship to attend the lycée. He passed, and was awarded the scholarship. Without this, the story might have been quite different, and might indeed never have been told. Madame Camus could never have afforded to send her son to school. Readers of Camus owe a great debt to that obscure schoolteacher. When, forty years later, Camus was awarded the Nobel Prize, his published speech of acceptance, *Discours de Suède*, was dedicated to M. Louis Germain.

From the age of ten to seventeen, Camus was at the lycée. As a scholarship boy from the slums, he mixed with fee-paying, properly-turned-out sons of middle-class families. He tells us almost nothing of this period. But we know that he discovered the joys of sport. He was an excellent swimmer. He danced better than anybody else. And, above all, he excelled in football. If we are to believe him, he spent these formative years not reading, but keeping goal. He rose to become the goalkeeper of a club called Racing Universitaire d'Alger. The love of football never left him. When famous, he was often to be seen

[1] See *Actuelles* III, p. 38.

among the Sunday afternoon crowd at a stadium. Football gave him his only lessons in ethics, he said.[1]

He also discovered the natural beauty of the open spaces, the release of the blue sky and the infinite sea. Most of his swimming was done in the clear, blue, empty Mediterranean. From all points of view, life now seemed to be good.

Tragedy struck at the very moment when it would be most acutely felt. Camus fell ill with tuberculosis, at the age of seventeen, and was sent to hospital. His studies were interrupted, his sport had to be abandoned. Even his life was no longer a certainty. In this cruel, direct way, the fragility of life, its lack of guarantee, was brought home to the young Camus. Henceforth, he was, quite understandably, to be preoccupied with health, robustness, and with the need to get the most out of life. Tuberculosis was never far away. It was to attack him at several important stages in his life. Yet it never made him bitter. In *L'Envers et L'Endroit*, Camus noted that serious illness had frightened him, discouraged him, but not embittered him.[2] Resentment was quite foreign to his nature. Quite the contrary, tuberculosis had the effect of strengthening his will to resist. At about this time Camus wrote: 'J'ai trop longtemps méconnu les forces de vitalité que je porte en moi . . . Je m'aperçois sans complaisance aucune que je suis capable de résistance – d'énergie – de volonté. . . . Mon état physique laisse, il est vrai, à désirer. Mais j'ai le désir de guérir.'[3]

The experience of a near fatal and unmerited illness confronted Camus very early with two stark truths – the truth of death and the will to resist it. Both aspects of the experience pulse throughout his writing as a constant presence.

When he recovered, Camus resumed his studies and in 1932 was admitted to the Faculté des Lettres d'Alger. At the same

[1] Pierre de Boisdeffre, *Métamorphose de la Littérature*, Vol. II, p. 260.
[2] p. 19.
[3] 'For too long I have not appreciated the power of vitality that I carry within me. I now realize, without complacency, that I am capable of resistance, of energy, of will-power. It is true that my physical condition leaves something to be desired. But I have the will to get better.' (BM) Quoted in Roger Quilliot's introduction to the *Pléiade* edition.

time, he left home and went to live alone. He supported himself by selling car accessories, working as a clerk in the Town Hall, and doing a variety of other odd jobs.

At the university, Camus was taught by the philosopher Jean Grenier (who had given him a few lessons before his illness). Camus was frequently to acknowledge the immense debt which he owed to Grenier for his intellectual formation. When Grenier's book *Les Iles* was published in 1933, Camus decided that he would be a writer. The two men became firm friends. Camus read voraciously, and thought constantly.

He married at the age of twenty, but divorced his wife the following year.

An idealist and a Socialist, Camus joined the Communist Party some time in 1934, and was entrusted with the task of spreading propaganda among the Muslim population. The following year, the Franco-Russian alliance which Laval[1] and Stalin signed in Moscow led to a change in Communist policy in Algeria. Camus was told to preach a different gospel. This exercise in political cynicism disgusted him, and he abruptly left the party. He was never to join another political party of any colour or persuasion. From that day, his politics remained resolutely independent.

Camus appears to have begun writing in 1935. In that year, he founded a theatrical company for young working-class people and called it the Théâtre du Travail. It was for this company that he wrote, ostensibly in collaboration with the cast, his first play, *Révolte dans les Asturies*. Based on a workers' uprising in Spain in 1934, it was a play with a very clear political message. At the same time, Camus was writing his essays collected under the title *L'Envers et L'Endroit* (published in 1937). He earned his living as an actor with the

[1] Alarmed by the growing power of Hitler in Germany, France sought alliances in eastern Europe at the beginning of 1935. Negotiations were opened with Russia, as a result of which France obtained Russia's admission to the League of Nations, and the two countries signed a Pact of Mutual Assistance on 2 May 1935. One of the side-effects of this pact was that Russia should cease spreading revolutionary propaganda in Algeria against French interests.

Radio-Alger group of strolling players. Camus often said that he was happiest among actors. He said that the theatre was the only place where one could be innocent, in the sense that one admitted one was playing a part, pretending, assuming emotions and thoughts. In the theatre, there was no dissembling in the hope that one would not be discovered; on the contrary, one dissembled openly, and hoped to be discovered. He found it an honest profession, said there was truth in the theatre and illusion in society, and many years later declared that he might have been happy had he remained an actor. He intended originally to play the part of Caligula in his own play of that name, but Gérard Philippe eventually took the role. It is certainly true that he was most relaxed with theatrical people, not with intellectuals. And it was to the theatre that he retreated in the fifties, after the calumnies that appeared in the press, and devoted his last years to a number of brilliant and highly successful theatrical adaptations. It is not generally known that he played one of the parts in his own adaptation of Faulkner's *Requiem for a Nun*, one evening when the actor who should have played the part was suddenly taken ill.

Like Molière, Camus was for a couple of years, in 1935–6, actor, adaptor, director, and inspiration of his Workers' Theatre.

At the same time, he completed his degree, and prepared a thesis on Neo-Platonism and Christian Thought. This essay will be considered in its place later, but it was clearly the first time Camus had examined Christianity in depth, and he seems already to feel a preference for the more human appeal of the Greeks; he remains, however, scrupulously objective in his thesis, despite a leaning which we, with hindsight, are able to detect. Poor health prevented Camus from presenting the thesis, and from this time, he abandoned any idea he might have had for an academic career.

His Workers' Theatre had meanwhile fallen into the hands of the Communist Party, which he distrusted for its opportunism. He rescued it, renamed it *Théâtre de l'Equipe*, and devoted himself to it almost full time in 1937, apart from some foreign trips, notably to Italy. In 1938, Camus started writing for the newspaper *Alger Républicain*, and it soon became apparent that he would henceforth make his living in journalism. He wrote literary reviews, political articles, editorials. He also wrote, in this year, his play *Caligula* and published his essays *Noces*. The first notes for a novel were penned. The first draft was called *Une Mort Heureuse*, which has been preserved and was recently published. The second version became a different novel: *L'Etranger*.

In the meantime, the international situation grew darker and darker. It was quite obvious that a devastating war was imminent. Camus went to Oran, where he met and married his second wife, Francine. When war was declared, he volunteered for service, more from a moral responsibility than from any political conviction. He was rejected, again on the grounds of his health. He went to Paris, worked on *Paris-Soir*, and after the invasion and German occupation went with the newspaper to Clermont-Ferrand. Then a brief period in Lyon, and back to Algeria.

The year 1941 was spent teaching in Algeria. At the end of that year, a capital event occurred. The Nazis executed Gabriel Péri, one of the leaders of the French Communist Party, and Camus, outraged, decided that he could no longer remain outside the struggle. He joined the resistance movement, and fought with the network known as 'Combat'. His health, for once, was not questioned. He started to write the now famous articles for the clandestine newspaper, also called *Combat*, which breathed such fire and spirit into the Resistance Movement. In 1942, his activities were interrupted by another serious attack of tuberculosis. Also in this year, *L'Etranger* was published. The little-known author who suddenly burst upon the scene with this extraordinary book, destined to be one of the key books of the age, was the same as the mysterious author of rousing, honest editorials in *Combat*, the man whom presumably the Nazis would dearly love to silence. But at the time, of course, no one knew.

*   *   *

Character

Albert Camus was invigorating, enlivening company. He was what I should call a 'life' person; his natural inclination was always towards what was joyful, positive, constructive, helpful, and fun. In conversation, he was not one to dwell upon misery and misfortune. He adored life with a passion which was admirable and enviable. He was seldom known to be downcast. Despite the first impression received by some readers from his books, and the reputation which has followed him, I think it is important to remember that Camus felt that life was to be lived, not to be talked about. His work is a hymn to life, written by one who knew so well how easily it could slip away. He embraced life fully, and never insulted it with a sardonic or impatient gesture of depreciation. In *L'Eté* he wrote, 'Il y a ainsi une volonté de vivre sans rien refuser de la vie qui est la vertu que j'honore le plus en ce monde.'[1]

Camus considered the love of life more important than the meaning of life. He agreed with Dostoïevsky's view that one must love life before its meaning, and he added that when the love of life disappears, no meaning can console. Therefore, we must ensure that our priorities are the right ones.

Obviously, a man such as I have described generated much warmth of character. He was always sympathetic, never remotely spiteful or triumphant. He had many friends, who knew that they could trust him without the matter ever being mentioned. He talked down to no one. He said that if he were to write a book on ethics, there would be 100 pages, out of which 99 would be blank. On the last page he would write, 'I know of only one duty, and that is to love.' (*Carnets*). It is a measure of the friendship which he aroused that after his death some of the proof-readers and typesetters who had worked with him joined together and themselves wrote a book devoted to his memory.

Camus was strict in his adherence to the truth. He was quite

[1] p. 166. 'Thus there is a will to live while refusing nothing of what life offers which is the virtue that I honour most in all this world.'

incapable of lying about any matter of importance, and he urged his fellows to find happiness in facing the truth about themselves and about the human condition. There was no peace in evasion of the truth, or in self-delusion. A wise man, he said, lives with what he has, without speculating on what he has not.

Part of the truth was that absolute justice was impossible, just as eternal love and eternal hate were impossible. While remaining an idealist in his hopes for mankind, he was none the less a realist in his assessment of their probable realization. But if justice was not possible all the time, one could certainly attempt to promote it some of the time. He was upset by cynics who found an excuse for injustice, hatred or scorn in the knowledge that the values of justice, love, and sympathy were relative.

Camus was writing at a time of severe and virulent partisan squabbles, a time of fanaticism, of poisonous propaganda, in the midst of which his was a voice of moderation and good sense, for which he was frequently reproached by those of his 'disciples' whose opinions were more frenetic. He was not a prejudiced man, in the sense that he did not pre-judge an issue. His opinions were empirical, never doctrinaire. The hatred engendered by obedience to an implacable doctrine appalled him. For his part, he never ceased to have respect for the opinion of others. He said that he could deny a view without feeling obliged to defile it, or to withdraw from others the right to believe it. It is refreshing to find a writer who rejected any temptation to proselytize. This is because Camus was rarely sure that he was right. Whereas others, notably Sartre, had reached conclusions, Camus did not cease to grope. He hesitated. He found contradictions in his own thought.[1] Having the ability to see all sides of a question, he was denied

---

[1] 'It's all the same to me if I find myself in contradiction. I don't wish to be a philosophic genius. I don't even want to be a genius at all, finding it hard enough to be a man. I want to find harmony and, knowing that I cannot kill myself, I want to know whether I can kill someone else or allow him to be killed, and I shall draw every consequence from my question, even if it means contradicting myself.' Private letter quoted in the introduction to the *Pléiade* edition, p. 1612 (BM).

the certainty of conviction. This makes for a degree of muddle-headed thinking in his non-fiction, but it has the virtue of honesty and the stamp of humility. On one occasion, after a public dispute with François Mauriac on a matter of principle, Camus later admitted publicly that Mauriac had been right, and he had been wrong. 'Est-ce qu'on peut faire le parti de ceux qui ne sont pas sûrs d'avoir raison?' he wrote. Ce serait le mien. Dans tous les cas, je n'insulte pas ceux qui ne sont pas avec moi. C'est ma seule originalité.'[1]

Camus wrote books because he could not bear that men should live with falsehood and oppression. He asked his readers to face facts, and to gain strength and joy from their lucidity. He did not regard himself as a philosopher or the leader of a movement. His aims were humbler, but they have their own grandeur, because they were imbued with a transparent sincerity.

> Mon rôle, je le reconnais, n'est pas de transformer le monde, ni l'homme; je n'ai pas assez de vertus, ni de lumières pour cela. Mais il est, peut-être, de servir à ma place, les quelques valeurs sans lesquelles un monde, même transformé, ne vaut pas la peine d'être vécu, sans lesquelles un homme, même nouveau, ne vaudra pas d'être respecté.[2]

* * *

First Writing

Camus's first attempt at sustained writing was not published until 1971 (and in translation in 1972), although it had been written in Algiers between 1936 and 1938. This was *La Mort Heureuse*. Its theme is the exultation of life, and the

[1] *Actuelles* I, p. 231. 'Is it possible to found a party for those who are not sure they are right? That would be my party. At all events, I do not insult those who are not on my side. That is my only originality.' (BM)

[2] *Actuelles* I, p. 206. 'I recognize that my role is not to transform the world, or man; I have neither the virtue nor the understanding for that. But it is perhaps to contribute my own part in serving those few values without which even a transformed world is not worth living in, without which even a new man will not deserve respect.' (BM)

examination of the problem how to live happily, so that one may die happily. The hero, Mersault, wants more than anything to avoid the ignominy and humiliation of a 'natural death', that is the death of the spirit while the body still lives, enslaved and oppressed by routines. He murders his mentor, Zagreus, in what is a deliberate, cold and calculated crime. The best scene in the book is the encounter between the two protagonists immediately before the murder. Zagreus is a helpless cripple. He has to be washed and dried by someone, whom he pays for this service. He is legless. Yet, in an impassioned speech, he proclaims his will to live in spite of physical debility:

> Je ne ferai jamais un geste pour abréger une vie à laquelle je crois tant. J'accepterais pis encore, aveugle, muet, tout ce que vous voudrez, pourvu seulement que je sente dans mon ventre cette flamme sombre et ardente qui est moi et moi vivant.[1]

It is impossible to resist the view that Camus is here speaking for himself. (Indeed, he did little else, for he was unable to create characters who were believable except as mouthpieces for opinion. Not one of his fictional creations lives with an independent existence.) Zagreus has no legs, Camus lived under the constant threat of tuberculosis, both have a sharper awareness of the simple value of being alive as a result of their handicaps. This is not the last time that Camus will treat the theme of physical debility.

Mersault appears to be unmoved by his victim's *credo*. He kills him. He is dimly aware that his own quest for happiness starts with that shot. He takes Zagreus's money, and begins his wandering through central Europe. Here the book becomes confused, loses direction. The tension and interest of the first part are not recaptured. There is a period in Prague, after which Mersault returns to Algiers, lives with three girls, marries another, moves, and dies of tuberculosis. The latter part of the

---

[1] p. 70. 'I shall never make the slightest move to shorten a life in which I believe so deeply. I would accept to be even worse off, blind, dumb, anything you like, providing only that I could feel in my belly that dark, ardent flame which is me and me alive.' (BM)

story is full of the ecstatic contemplation of the beauty of the earth, against which the hero's own disgusting illness appears as an unjustifiable obscenity. Only when he dies, joins the 'immobile world', and loses himself in the cosmos, does he achieve his destiny.

Other themes occur which will be developed later in Camus's work. There is an unmistakable anger at the corroding influence of poverty, which must become as ruthless as the system which invented and maintains it, if it is to defend itself. Here Camus is thinking of his mother, and his neighbours in the slums of Algiers:

> Cette malédiction sordide et révoltante selon laquelle les pauvres finissent dans la misère la vie qu'ils ont commencée dans la misère, il (Mersault) l'avait rejetée en combattant l'argent par l'argent, avec la haine la haine.[1]

There is, in *La Mort Heureuse*, a subsidiary theme, barely discernible, which touches upon Camus's unavowed distrust of women, of their duplicity and their cunning. It is not an idea which holds a large place in his work, although it is perhaps significant that among female characters, only Marthe in *Le Malentendu* is given any real identity; all other major characters are men. (Camus had divorced his first wife one year before writing *La Mort Heureuse*.)

* * *

Camus's next work, and the first to be published, was *L'Envers et L'Endroit* (1937). The book consists of five essays, some of which resemble short stories, in which Camus uses disguised autobiography to meditate upon certain themes. He maintained that he was not satisfied with the literary quality of the book, and did not allow a second edition until 1958. At the same time, he acknowledged that this immature work contained the essence in embryo of all his subsequent writing, which was a development of preoccupations expressed in these

[1] p. 184. 'Mersault had rejected that sordid and revolting curse according to which the poor must finish in misery a life they have begun in misery, by fighting money with money, hatred with hatred.' (BM)

early essays. Those preoccupations are with the pitiful loneliness of old age, with the irony of man's tragic condition of
suffering and pointless death played out against a décor of
beauty and majesty, with the cancer of inescapable poverty,
and with the fraudulence of religious consolation. Above all,
L'Envers et L'Endroit contains a youthful expression of love,
an aspect of Camus's writing which is frequently passed over.
'Il y a plus de véritable amour dans ces pages maladroites
que dans toutes celles qui ont suivi', wrote Camus in his
preface years later.[1] It is true, these pages testify to a deeply
felt and moving compassion, illustrated by a collection of
neglected people whose lives are banal, lonely, desperate. The
first essay, *Irony*, shows an old woman who is abandoned by
her younger companions who prefer to spend the evening at
the cinema; she is left to her solitary contemplations. An old
man tries to keep the attention of the young by telling stories.
But he suffers the ultimate pain of realizing that no one is
listening to him, that one by one they have left him to talk to
himself, that he is a bore, useless and in the way. They imply
that the least he can do, while waiting to die, is to shut up.
The old woman, meanwhile, unable to stand her solitude, takes
refuge in religion. She turns to God through fear, not love, for
protection from the horror of neglect. But if men did not
neglect her, she would soon abandon her statues, her beads and
her mumblings. In a striking phrase, Camus says that even
God cannot assuage her loneliness for long, for her religion is
this 'tête-à-tête décevant avec Dieu'.[2] Again, misquoting Pascal
with pointed irony, Camus says that the old woman suffers
'la misère de l'homme en Dieu'.[3]

---

[1] p. 13. 'There is more genuine love in these clumsy pages than in all
the others which have followed them.'

[2] 'disappointing chat with God.' (BM)

[3] 'the misery of man with God.' (BM). Blaise Pascal (1623–62) was a
deeply religious philosopher and mathematician. His *Pensées* are a collection of notes for a book which he was preparing, to be called *Apologie de la
Religion Chrétienne*. One of his themes was to contrast the poverty of man
without God ('la misère de l'homme sans Dieu') with the richness and
grandeur of man who strives towards the infinite.

Camus's attitude towards the illusory comfort of the old woman in religion is not angry, triumphant, or bitter. He has sympathy and understanding, which on the contrary are deepened by the fact that her lonely quest for solace goes unheeded by the great metaphysical silence.

Silence is likewise the theme of the second essay, *Entre Oui et Non*, which is the portrait of a mother, poor but dignified, silent and uncommunicative. Again, it is the ability to *feel* deeply which the reader recognizes. These essays could not have been written by a cold, logical thinker.

The third and fourth essays describe the sense of strangeness which comes with foreign travel, the feeling of alienation and the intimation of what it means to be an 'outsider' in life. The last essay explains the title of the book. *L'envers* is the right side up, on a piece of cloth; *l'endroit* is the other side. The world which Camus contemplates also has its duality; there is the beauty of nature, the warmth of the sun, which make one rejoice, and there is the suffering of men, which makes one despair. You cannot have the one sensation without the other; they go hand in hand, and intensify each other. 'Il n'y a pas amour de vivre sans désespoir de vivre.'[1] The first statement of what was later to become the ethic of consciousness in the Absurd, is to be found in these pages of a young man, who, at the age of twenty-two had already seen and experienced enough of life to know that it required courage to be lived:

> J'avais besoin d'une grandeur. Je la trouvais dans la confrontation de mon désespoir profond et de l'indifférence secrète d'un des plus beaux paysages du monde. J'y puisais la force d'être courageux et conscient à la fois.'[2]

We must accept the contradictions inherent in life. We cannot

[1] p. 107. 'There is no love of life without despair of life.'
[2] p. 94. 'I needed a greatness. I found it in the confrontation between my deep despair and the secret indifference of one of the most beautiful landscapes in the world. I drew from it the strength to be at one and the same time both courageous and aware.'

expect a disordered world to give order to human existence. We must face up to the truth, that death is the ultimate trick played upon us, and that it makes nonsense of any attempt to give 'meaning' to life. We can at least preserve for ourselves a certain lucidity, a refusal to tell lies or listen to them. Then we can love life, embrace it for all we are worth, and live 'as if' it meant something.

> je n'aime pas qu'on triche. Le grand courage, c'est encore de tenir les yeux ouverts sur la lumière comme sur la mort. Au reste, comment dire le lien qui mène de cet amour dévorant de la vie à ce désespoir secret. Si j'écoute l'ironie, tapie au fond des choses, elle se découvre lentement. Clignant son oeil petit et clair: 'Vivez comme si . . .', dit-elle. Malgré bien des recherches, c'est là toute ma science.'[1]

* * *

About 1937, Camus wrote a play, *Caligula*, which was not performed until 1944, and which will be considered later. His next published work was four essays under the collective title *Noces* (1938). Camus told Jean-Claude Brisville that he had had moments of doubt after the writing of *L'Envers et L'Endroit*. He was not sure whether he would write again.[2] Then a passionate love of life exploded within him, and cried for expression. That is when he wrote *Noces*. Indeed, it is an intensely lyrical exaltation of the natural world, of the sun-drenched landscape of his native Algeria, of the life of the senses. Camus never wrote a more sensual book. The 'noces' in the title are the nuptials between man and the earth. The author actually feels the joy of the earth against his body, of the

---

[1] p. 119. 'I don't like people to cheat. Great courage still consists of gazing steadfastly at the light as on death. Besides, how can I define the thread which leads from this all-consuming love of life to this secret despair. If I listen to the voice of irony, crouching underneath things, it slowly shows itself. Winking its small, clear eye: "Live as if . . ." In spite of much searching, that is all I know.'

[2] Jean-Claude Brisville, *Camus*, p. 256.

sea flowing over it. This leads to a hymn of praise to the present, to the sensual pleasure of 'now'. Camus rejects any promise of 'tomorrow', and especially the religious promise of an after-life. He refuses to devalue the richness of the present, or the enjoyment thereof, by contemplating an unknowable future. That death makes the concept of 'future' absurd, is all the more reason to embrace fully the present, physically as well as intellectually.

There is no suggestion of a pantheistic approach in this celebration of nature. Camus does not entertain any hope that nature may have a spiritual identity, or may console us for the absence of any meaning to life. In fact, far from consoling, nature makes the meaninglessness of human life more intense and more difficult to bear, as nature is permanent and self-perpetuating, whereas we who contemplate it are inexorably finite. But we must accept this state of affairs, and not construct in our imagination a life other than the one we have. Sin, for Camus, would be to denigrate the life that we have and invent a better one, to refuse the present and hope for a future. Sin in the conventional Christian sense is not within Camus's experi-ence. That is not to say that it is beyond his comprehension, since he had already by now written his thesis on Plotinus and Christianity and had examined Christian theology more deeply than most of us, as an examination of the 60,000-word text, reprinted in the Pléiade edition, will show. Here, no detail is missed in his effort to understand and interpret, the refer-ences from Biblical sources are apposite and abundant, the style scrupulously objective, the bibliography extensive.[1] But he now sets aside the question as unworthy of human deliber-ance. Dr Cruickshank is surely wrong, then, to talk of Camus's 'naïve atheism'.[2] He mistakes what is uncomplicated for what is unreflected. Camus's view is certainly refreshingly simple. It can be summarized as follows: we must be honest and face the truth. The truth is that the human condition is mortal. Also, it is the only reality of which we can be sure. Therefore, if we

[1] *Essais*, Bibliothèque de la Pléiade, pp. 1224–1313.
[2] John Cruickshank, *Albert Camus and the Literature of Revolt*, p. 36.

are to find happiness, which every man wants, then we must find it in this mortal life, and not look for it elsewhere, in which case we would be bound to be disappointed. In this way, we are being candid with ourselves, and loyal to our condition. Any promise of religious consolation can be no more than an idea, and we do not have to live with ideas. Such is Camus's religious position as revealed in *Noces*. It was to undergo some modifications later, but at this time, he saw it as a joyful expression of pagan Algerian pleasure in life, a pleasure which regards the traditional Christian obsessions with sin, punishment, and resignation, as anti-human, sterile, and irrelevant.

Camus's experience of the world, and his resultant attitude towards life, must be regarded equally as valid as a religious experience, which results in contrary conclusions. It cannot be dismissed as 'naïve', at least no more than a belief in the resurrection of a dead human body. On the other hand, Camus does take it for granted that spiritual comfort is an illusion. He does not investigate the possibility that it might make life, here and now, more enjoyable. Camus recognizes that there are those who would make such a claim, but he would regard them as avoiding the necessity of facing life squarely, with all its imperfections and injustices. They are turning their backs on life.

2

L'Etranger

Albert Camus's first books attracted little attention. When *L'Etranger* was published in 1942, however, the author found himself suddenly famous. The book was an immediate success, giving expression in a supremely chiselled fictional form to a *malaise* and an anxiety which were characteristic of a whole generation. To this day, those who read the novel in 1942 recall the powerful revelatory effect that it had. It was one of those literary events which are the relish of French intellectuals.

It must not be forgotten that Camus was not writing for intellectuals, nor did he enjoy being lionized by them. As in his first books, he was concerned with the little man, whose sufferings went unnoticed, who was inarticulate, introverted, discontented in silence. In writing this novel, Camus was speaking for all those who could not speak for themselves. He made this quite clear by choosing a hero who was insignificant, inoffensive, unremarkable, a nonentity working in an office. And the story is told in the first person, in the kind of spare, economic style that such a person would adopt. It is quite devoid of metaphorical colour, imagination, or reflection. *L'Etranger* is the story of a man who has lived a life of the senses, in total simplicity and innocent enjoyment, but whom Society eventually roots out, humiliates, and crushes.

Meursault is employed in an office in Algiers. At the very beginning of the narrative, he learns that his mother has died, either that day or the day before, he is not quite sure. He received a telegram from the home in which he had placed her which said, laconically, 'Mère décédée. Enterrement demain. Sentiments distingués.'[1] At the funeral, he does not weep. The

---

[1] 'Your mother passed away. Funeral tomorrow. Deep sympathy.'

next day, he goes swimming, meets a girl whom he used to know, Marie, takes her to the cinema and then to his bed. His neighbour, a pimp called Raymond Masson, is having trouble with a former mistress, an Arab girl, and is being pursued by two Arab men who want to avenge her for his treatment of her. Raymond asks Meursault to write a letter on his behalf; Meursault obliges. The following Sunday, Meursault, Marie and Raymond run into the two Arabs on the beach, there is a fight, and Raymond is wounded. Later, Meursault comes across the Arabs again, quite by chance, on the beach. He is carrying Raymond's revolver. Blinded by the sun, but quite without provocation, Meursault shoots one of the men, then fires another three bullets into the prostrate body. He is arrested and tried. In the course of the trial, the counsel for the prosecution presents as evidence Meursault's conduct at his mother's funeral and his subsequent behaviour with Marie, and establishes that his criminal nature is demonstrated. The jury finds him guilty, and he is condemned to death. In the cell, he refuses angrily the consolations offered by the priest, because he does not believe in God, but does believe in the life of which he is about to be deprived. He realizes for the first time how much he has loved life, however ridiculous and meaningless it may have been. He accepts his destiny with clear understanding.

Before the chain of events which lead to his arrest and trial, Meursault's awareness of life is severely limited. He is affected by a profoundly apathetic *ennui*, which makes him uncommonly sensitive to the dullness and monotony of existence. Though he does not say so, the reader feels that he sees very little point in life, but merely carries on for want of anything better to do. He sleeps, eats, works, all without enthusiasm, and observes with detachment the mechanical gestures with which people fill their lives. He sees around him nothing but sterile routine. The people who form the décor to the story, and these include Meursault himself, do not wonder, question, or think. Both inwardly and outwardly, their existence is dominated by habit.

One of the most effective passages in which Camus gives the *feeling* of this deadening predictability of the day's events is that which describes the interdependent relationship of the old man, Salamano, and his mangy dog, whom he beats and curses, but is used to:

> Ils ont l'air de la même race et pourtant ils se détestent. Deux fois par jour, à onze heures et à six heures, le vieux mène son chien promener. Depuis huit ans, ils n'ont pas changé leur itinéraire. On peut les voir le long de la rue de Lyon, le chien tirant l'homme jusqu'à ce que le vieux Salamano bute. Il bat son chien alors et il l'insulte. Le chien rampe de frayeur et se laisse traîner. A ce moment, c'est au vieux de le tirer. Quand le chien a oublié, il entraîne de nouveau son maître et il est de nouveau battu et insulté. Alors ils restent tous les deux sur le trottoir et ils se regardent, le chien avec terreur, l'homme avec haine. C'est ainsi tous les jours . . . Il y a huit ans que cela dure.[1]

That Meursault is by no means free from this kind of torpor is clear from his remarks on the evening after his mother's funeral:

> J'ai pensé que c'était toujours un dimanche de tiré, que maman était maintenant enterrée, que j'allais reprendre mon travail et que, somme toute, il n'y avait rien de changé.[2]

If we remember that the hero of *La Mort Heureuse* was similarly afflicted with boredom, and wanted more than anything

---

[1] p. 44. 'But, oddly enough, though so much alike, they detest each other. Twice a day, at eleven and six, the old fellow takes his dog for a walk, and for eight years that walk has never varied. You can see them in the Rue de Lyon, the dog pulling his master along as hard as he can, till finally the old chap misses a step and nearly falls. Then he beats his dog and calls it names. The dog cowers and lags behind, and it's his master's turn to drag him along. Presently the dog forgets, starts tugging at the leash again, gets another hiding and more abuse. Then they halt on the pavement, the pair of them, and glare at each other; the dog with terror and the man with hatred in his eyes. Every time they're out this happens. . . . It's been going on like this for eight years.'

[2] p. 41. 'It occurred to me that somehow I'd got through another Sunday, that Mother now was buried, and tomorrow I'd be going back to work as usual. Really, nothing in my life had changed.'

to escape a living death, and that the old people Camus described with such concern in *L'Envers et L'Endroit* were dying of entrenched habit, it becomes obvious that the author regards monotony as the greatest single cause of unhappiness among men. To suggest, as some critics have, that Meursault is 'happy' before his crime is wrong; he is too taciturn for such a positive emotion (although he does admit with typical indifference, that he cannot exactly be called 'unhappy', p. 58).

The only real pleasure that he knows is sensual pleasure, the colour of the bay, the embrace of cool air as relief from the burning sun, the sweep of the waves over his tired body. Here again we rediscover themes from the earlier books. Satisfaction is derived from the gratification of the senses. 'A travers les lignes de cyprès qui menaient aux collines près du ciel, cette terre rousse et verte, ces maisons rares et bien dessinées...'[1] 'La même campagne lumineuse gorgée de soleil.'[2] 'J'avais tout le ciel dans les yeux et il était bleu et doré.'[3] 'J'avais laissé ma fenêtre ouverte et c'était bon de sentir la nuit d'été couler sur nos corps bruns.'[4] The lyrical sensuality of *Noces* is recalled by the description of Meursault, Raymond Masson and Marie on the beach:

> Sur la plage, je me suis étendu à plat ventre près de Masson et j'ai mis ma figure dans le sable. Je lui ai dit que 'c'était bon' et il était de cet avis. Peu après, Marie est venue. Je me suis retourné pour la regarder avancer. Elle était toute visqueuse d'eau salée et elle tenait ses cheveux en arrière. Elle s'est allongée flanc à flanc avec moi et les deux chaleurs de son corps et du soleil m'ont un peu endormi.[5]

[1] p. 33. '. . . the long lines of cypresses sloping up towards the skyline and the hills, the hot red soil dappled with vivid green, and here and there a lonely house sharply outlined against the light.'

[2] p. 34. 'The same sun-drenched countryside.'

[3] p. 37. 'I had the sky full in my eyes, all blue and gold.'

[4] p. 52. 'I'd left my window open and it was pleasant to feel the cool night air flowing over our sunburnt bodies.'

[5] p. 67. 'When I made the beach I stretched myself belly-downwards beside Masson, resting my face on the sand. I told him "it was fine" here and he agreed. Presently Marie came back. I raised my head to watch her

The most important characteristic of these simple, spontaneous pleasures is that they are rooted in the present. Meursault lives entirely for what he is feeling now; he does not remember what he felt yesterday, nor does he anticipate what he will feel tomorrow. His life is a succession of unrelated instants, valuable in themselves, but losing all value when they are over. Not looking backwards, he cannot know remorse. Not looking forwards, he cannot know hope. These words are to him empty generalities. This is why, when Marie asks him if he loves her, he says that the question is meaningless. 'Love' as she understands it involves permanence, a commitment to the future. Meursault knows that no one can predict what he will feel in the future, and so the question cannot honestly be answered. She asks him if he would like to marry her. He says that it is all the same to him, but they could if she wanted to. He is not thinking of a continuing emotion; he is thinking no further than of what she may like to hear *now*.

We can now begin to see why the novel is called *L'Etranger*. For, after all, a person who limits himself to the present tense is unusual. He is a 'stranger' among his fellows, with their pasts and their futures, their regrets and their aspirations. Being so unlike them, so 'bizarre' as Marie puts it, he is exiled and alone. Every time he opens his mouth he declares himself, unwittingly, an exile in society. If we were to meet him, we should say that he was always 'putting his foot in it', and embarrassing us by saying the wrong thing. In truth, as we shall see later, it is not so much that he says the wrong thing, as that he says everything. It is his unselective honesty that makes us uncomfortable. He is an 'outsider' because he acts in accordance with his sentiments in a society where it is expected that other considerations should govern one's behaviour.

Camus conveys the impression of his hero's strangeness first by showing how he sees other people, and then by showing

approach. She was glistening with brine and holding her hair back. Then she lay down beside me and what with the combined warmth of our bodies and the sun, I felt myself dropping off to sleep.'

how others see him. When Meursault observes others, he does
so from the outside, without intuitive comprehension, aided
by experience, which one would normally bring to bear in one's
assessment of people. He talks as if he has never seen people
before, as if they were from an alien world:

> Je n'avais encore jamais remarqué à quel point les vieilles
> femmes pouvaient avoir du ventre. Les hommes étaient
> presque tous très maigres et tenaient des cannes. Ce qui me
> frappait dans leurs visages, c'est que je ne voyais pas leurs
> yeux, mais seulement une lueur sans éclat au milieu d'un
> nid de rides. . . . De temps en temps seulement, j'entendais
> un bruit singulier et je ne pouvais comprendre ce qu'il
> était. A la longue, j'ai fini par deviner que quelques-uns
> d'entre les vieillards suçaient l'intérieur de leurs joues et
> laissaient échapper ces clappements bizarres.[1]

As for the attitude of others towards him, Marie finds him odd,
his own counsel finds him positively repellent: 'Il m'a regardé
d'une façon bizarre, comme si je lui inspirais un peu de
dégoût.'[2] 'Il ne me comprenait pas et il m'en voulait un peu.'[3]
The judge comes no closer to understanding him; he tells him
that he has never met such a hardened soul (p. 85). In court,
Meursault finally recognizes his own strangeness, and, piti-
fully, shows a rare sign of emotion: 'j'ai eu une envie stupide de
pleurer parce que j'ai senti combien j'étais détesté par tous ces
gens-là'[4] And he notices the fact that the trial seems to take
place without his participation (p. 111). The prosecutor has,

---

[1] pp. 27–9. 'I'd never yet noticed what big paunches old women usually
have. Most of the men, however, were thin as rakes, and they all carried
sticks. What struck me most about their faces was that one couldn't see
their eyes, only a dull glow in a sort of nest of wrinkles. . . . The only
sound was a rather queer one; it came at longish intervals, and at first I
was puzzled by it. However, after listening attentively, I guessed what it
was; the old men were sucking at the insides of their cheeks, and this
caused the odd, wheezing noises that had mystified me.'

[2] p. 81. 'He gave me a queer look, as if I slightly revolted him.'

[3] p. 82. 'He couldn't make me out and, naturally enough, this irritated
him.'

[4] p. 103. 'I had a foolish desire to burst into tears. For the first time I'd
realized how all these people loathed me.'

quite naturally, the most outraged reaction to Meursault. He calls him a 'monster', and declares that 'je n'avais rien à faire avec une société dont je méconnaissais les règles les plus essentielles et que je ne pouvais pas en appeler à ce cœur humain dont j'ignorais les réactions élémentaires.'[1]

Is the public prosecutor right? Is Meursault a monster? It is not an easy question. There is a disturbing ambiguity about the character, which makes it possible to return to the book time and time again with renewed enjoyment. Yet the reader never *quite* understands him, still less is able to judge him. It should be possible, however, to see why this simple, modest, self-effacing, inoffensive clerk should excite such loathing and fear in the court. It is certainly not simply because he has killed an Arab. In Algeria before the war it was inconceivable that a European, however poor, should be punished for the murder of an Arab, especially if he could plead self-defence. Judged simply in terms of believable narrative, *L'Etranger* would carry little conviction.

Meursault's own assessment of himself is that he is perfectly ordinary, 'absolument comme tout le monde'.[2] Since he is so obviously mistaken in this view, we may conclude that his powers of introspection are limited. He admits that he has very little imagination (p. 124), which would account for his inability to see why his attitudes cause distress. He is inarticulate, incapable of the customary colourful exaggeration which would lend emphasis to a statement. He is also extraordinarily passive. He does not initiate events, he reacts to them, in so far as they affect him at all. His language scarcely reflects an opinion on anything, or even an interest; it merely records facts. He allows himself to be drawn into a sequence of events which end in disaster, quite without volition. Everything happens to him by chance. He is for ever saying 'ça m'est égal', or 'ce n'était pas de ma faute', and he is right. Even his crime is not really

---

[1] p. 114. 'This man has no place in a community whose basic principles he flouts without compunction. Nor, heartless as he is, has he any claim to mercy.'

[2] p. 82. 'I was just like everybody else.'

committed by him. It is the fault of the sun. Camus insists on the power of the sun in the tense pages leading to the murder, a power which is relentless and which finally robs Meursault of whatever shreds of responsibility he may have had. Reacting only to his sensations of the moment, to the pain in his head caused by the overpowering sun, and the glint of steel which he dimly perceives in the Arab's hands, he shoots. 'It was because of the sun,' he says, and again, that is a perfectly accurate statement of fact.

Meursault's passivity is so total that he is wholly indifferent to the relative importance of courses of action which are proposed to him. Drinking a cup of coffee or going to bed with Marie have the same significance in his mind. There is no hierarchy of values. He restricts himself to answering questions, never affirms a choice. He accepts to write Raymond's letter for him, not out of generosity, but because he sees no reason not to; he does not weigh the likely merits or consequences of such an act (p. 49). He does not intervene when Raymond is bullied and struck by the policeman (p. 53); indifferent even to the distress of his neighbour, he stands aside and watches. When old Salamano, distraught at having lost his dog, bewails his pain, Meursault thinks that he must go to bed because he has got to get up early in the morning (p. 56). And, as we have seen, he does not care whether or not he marries Marie.

There is one area in which Meursault's instincts are entirely laudable, and that is his absolute and unshakeable refusal to lie about his own feelings, even when such a lie would save his skin and make him appear in a more comfortable light to the court. Were he to show the same hypocrisy as his accusers (an hypocrisy which has grown so habitual as to be almost unwilful), they would not feel that he was so alien and would not need to expel him from their midst, like a foreign object. It is important to notice that with the accusers, the tribal identity has taken over, and the conformist members of the tribe co-operate to eliminate the nonconformist who threatens, by his nonconformity, the very basis of their unity. Meursault is adamant in his strict adherence to the truth, so far as his own feelings and thoughts are concerned. He will not pretend to emotions that he does not have. He thereby reveals himself as the 'stranger', the 'intruder', the 'interloper' who has entered the territorial group from the outside and does not belong. It must be admitted that a man like Meursault would seem an outsider in almost any society, he would excite antagonism and aggression in us all. We all assume feelings, points of view, reactions, that are more or less manufactured, and take it for granted that we must lie or exaggerate to some extent every day. All except Meursault. He is consistently loyal to the truth of his own feelings, this being the only truth that he can know, that he can be sure about. Take from Meursault his sincerity, and he would crumple in vacuity.

He admits that his mother was bored when he went to see her at the Home, and that it took up his Sunday, without counting the effort required to catch the bus and to travel for two hours (p. 23). He says he would have gone to the country more often 'if it weren't for Mother', not because he resents her being a nuisance, or because he has no affection for her, but because it is a true statement of fact (p. 30). Talking to his own lawyer, he is uncompromisingly honest:

> Sans doute, j'aimais bien maman, mais cela ne voulait rien dire. Tous les êtres sains avaient plus ou moins souhaité la mort de ceux qu'ils aimaient. Ici l'avocat m'a coupé et a paru très agité. Il m'a fait promettre de ne pas dire cela à l'audience, ni chez le magistrat instructeur. Cependant, je lui ai expliqué que j'avais une telle nature que mes besoins physiques dérangeaient souvent mes sentiments. Le jour où j'avais enterré maman, j'étais très fatigué et j'avais sommeil. De sorte que je ne me suis pas rendu compte de ce qui se passait. Ce que je pouvais dire à coup sûr, c'est que j'aurais préféré que maman ne mourût pas. Mais mon avocat n'avait pas l'air content. Il m'a dit: 'Ceci n'est pas assez.'[1]

[1] p. 81. 'I could truthfully say that I'd been quite fond of Mother – but really that didn't mean much. All normal people, I added, as an after-thought, had more or less desired the death of those they loved, at some time or another. Here the lawyer interrupted me, looking greatly perturbed. "You must promise me not to say anything of that sort at the trial, or to

When asked if he has anything to say at his trial, he points out, quite gratuitously, that the prosecution witness is right to say that he offered him a cigarette at the morgue. He says so because it is true.

We are dealing here with a complete innocent. I do not wish to suggest that Meursault does not know he is telling the truth. He obviously recognizes the difference between truth and false-hood, but it is a distinction which he makes *for himself*, not in accordance with an imposed moral code. He does not tell the truth because he has been told that he should, but because it would be meaningless for him to do anything else. He is inno-cent in the sense that he is harmless, unaware of the injury which his truth might do to himself or the discomfort which it might cause others. It is an innocence untouched by Original Sin; Meursault has no Christian sense of guilt whatever. His truth is not only amoral – it is anterior to any concept of morals. There is in this sincerity a certain ingenuousness or lack of guile which reminds one of a child. Children have the same faculty of detachment from the implications or likely consequences of what they say. Camus was more explicit in his description of this child-like nature when describing the earlier hero, Mersault, in *La Mort Heureuse:*

> Alors, Mersault s'aperçut que pas une seule fois depuis Vienne il n'avait songé à Zagreus comme à l'homme qu'il avait tué de ses mains. Il reconnut en lui cette faculté d'oubli qui n'appartient qu'à l'enfant, au génie et à l'innocent.[1]

---

the examining magistrate." I promised, to satisfy him; but I explained that my physical condition at any given moment often influenced my feelings. For instance, on the day I attended Mother's funeral, I was fagged out and only half awake. So really I hardly took stock of what was happening. Anyhow I could assure him of one thing: that I'd rather Mother hadn't died. The lawyer, however, looked displeased. "That's not enough," he said curtly.'

[1] p. 125. 'Mersault then realized that not once since Vienna had he though of Zagreus as of the man he had killed with his own hands. He recognized in himself that capacity to forget which one finds only with the child, the genius, and the innocent.' (BM)

Meursault's innocence is too restricted to understand or deal with the traditional abstractions with which Society protects itself. It implicitly denies all accepted *a priori* rules of conduct and remains obstinately true to itself. Society has no alternative but to make a sacrificial victim of Meursault whose very presence places customary values in doubt. Camus wishes the reader to see that the morality which condemns Meursault is hypocritical and cruel. As he writes in *Le Mythe de Sisyphe*, 'J'ai vu des gens mal agir avec beaucoup de morale et je constate tous les jours que l'honnêteté n'a pas besoin de règles.'[1]

The accusers are shocked by Meursault's apparent calm at the death of his mother. He should have wept, he should have fallen upon her tomb, he should have suffered in mourning. He should not have smoked a cigarette after seeing the body, he should not have gone swimming, or to the cinema. He should not have enjoyed carnal pleasure. He did not, in short, play the role of the dutiful distressed son. He did not fabricate a continuity of feeling. Meursault is condemned for not behaving as others do; the murder he has committed is almost forgotten amid the indignation of his nonconformist conduct. Perhaps Meursault loved his mother, but he should have *shown* that he loved her. Society demands a display of sensitivity.

Society also demands some show of regret, some hint of contrition, some glimmer of ambition. Meursault, in his innocence, will not oblige. Society expects each member to share its myths, respect its idols, and treat its religion with suitable awe. Meursault can do none of this. The judge asks him if he believes in God, and is indignant when Meursault says that he does not. But everyone believes in God, he cries, even those who think they do not. Later, the priest shows the same incredulity in the face of the prisoner's independence of mind. Meursault has so far refused the chaplain's visits, because he does not believe in God. Are you quite sure? asks the priest. Meursault does not have to ruminate upon it, he says, it is not

[1] 'I have seen people with much moral support behaving very badly, and every day I notice that honesty has no need of rules.' (BM)

a question of any importance. He is condemned to death; he has not much time left, and he does not care to waste it with an hypothesis like God. Have you then no hope and do you live with the thought that you are going to die totally and completely, asks the priest. Yes, says Meursault (p. 128). The priest thinks he must be speaking like this because he is in despair. No, he is not. He is afraid, but that is all.

> 'Non, je ne peux pas vous croire. Je suis sûr qu'il vous est arrivé de souhaiter une autre vie.' Je lui ai répondu que naturellement, mais cela n'avait pas plus d'importance que de souhaiter d'être riche, de nager très vite ou d'avoir une bouche mieux faite. C'était du même ordre.[1]

Meursault is not being provocative in refusing Society's myth: once again, he is being honest, and innocent. In the same way as his ethical attitude is not so much amoral as pre-moral, so his lack of religious feeling is not anti-Christian but pre-Christian. He shows himself most irremediably an outsider by his admission that his actions are not necessarily motivated. People like to believe in causal connections; it is important that they should think their actions are purposive, that they do something because they have been motivated by a desire to do it, or because they hope thereby to achieve something else. Meursault reminds them that this is not true. His character, his behaviour, and his crime, all emphasize the part of irrationality in the human condition. Meursault shows that the immediate senses can dictate human behaviour as much as logical decision. This is a truth which Society cannot afford to face. There must always be a reason, not simply an explanation, otherwise upon what logic is the social organism based? The reader can feel the judge's anxiety, worry and blank incomprehension when he tries desperately to coax from Meursault the reasons for his act:

[1] p. 130. '"No! No! I refuse to believe it. I'm sure you've often wished there was an after-life." Of course I had, I told him. Everybody has that wish at times. But that had no more importance than wishing to be rich, or to swim very fast, or to have a better-shaped mouth. It was in the same order of things.'

Il s'est assis, a fourragé dans ses cheveux, a mis ses coudes sur son bureau et s'est penché un peu vers moi avec un air étrange: 'Pourquoi, pourquoi avez-vous tiré sur un corps à terre?' Là encore, je n'ai pas su répondre. Le juge a passé ses mains sur son front et a répété sa question d'une voix un peu altérée: 'Pourquoi? Il faut que vous me le disiez. Pourquoi?' Je me taisais toujours.[1]

The explanation for the crime is simple; it is that the sun was burning Meursault's eyes, branding his forehead, and distorting his vision. As for the *reason* why he shot the Arab, there simply is none. Meursault's story reminds us that there need not be a reason for everything. Hence Camus's scrupulous avoidance of causal conjunctions in Meursault's vocabulary. Restricting himself to a chronological description of events, he does not use words like 'because' or 'since'. Sentences do not follow upon each other in a logical chain. They succeed each other, almost without apparent connection. The conjunctions which Meursault uses are 'and' and 'then', words which give no hint of motivation.[2]

At the close of the book, Meursault's language abruptly changes. From being a passive spectator of life, he suddenly becomes a passionate advocate of life. Prodded by the persistence of the chaplain, he bursts into an angry, ecstatic affirmation of the one value he cherishes, which is life. It is his first, and only, positive statement. The final two paragraphs of the book are the culminating, joyous expression of Camus's own passionate love of life. '. . . il y a quelque chose qui a crevé en moi',[3] says Meursault, and there open the flood-gates on an anger and frustration with a world where the values of pretence,

---

[1] pp. 83–4. 'The magistrate kept fidgeting, running his fingers through his hair, half rising, then sitting down again. Finally, planting his elbows on the desk, he bent towards me with a queer expression. "But why, *why* did you go on firing at a prostrate man?" Again I found nothing to reply. The magistrate drew his hand across his forehead and repeated in a slightly different tone: "I ask you *why*, I insist on your telling me." I still kept silent.'

[2] See Cruickshank, op. cit., p. 155, and Jean-Paul Sartre, *Situations* I, p. 118.

[3] 'Something seemed to break inside me.'

self-delusion, falsehood and retribution are prized above those of honesty and tolerance. Paradoxically, he can face death now, because he has realized how much he loves life; the chaplain, on the other hand, who is already 'dead', does not love life – he prefers to wish for something better. Meursault, now lucid, aggressive and happy, accepts to die because he has lived, not because he hopes for an after-life. 'Je m'ouvrais pour la première fois à la tendre indifférence du monde.'[1]

Meursault goes to his death at his moment of conscious realization that, though life be absurd, it must be lived. It is his moment of revolt. Camus will use the end of *L'Etranger* as the starting-point for later books.

One matter which must be considered is the question as to whether or not Meursault's final affirmation is indeed a moment of revelation. Philip Thody believes that, on the contrary, Meursault is fully conscious throughout the book of the value of the attitude he represents,[2] and that he is merely goaded into making a public proclamation of this secret attitude by the persistence of the chaplain. Thody cites Camus himself as agreeing with this view. As Camus had an odd and mischievous habit of agreeing with whichever critic of his books he happened to be talking to, he is not always the best ally to invoke. Such an interpretation implies either hypocrisy or stupidity on Meursault's part, both of which are entirely out of keeping with the book. Were Meursault as clear-sighted, as passionate, and as assertive at the beginning of his tale as he is in the death-cell, he would presumably have shown none of the apathy, indifference, insensitivity with which his conduct is marked. Once one is lucid, it is not easy to stifle that lucidity and become bewildered, which is what Meursault would need to do if he were to fit Thody's interpretation. The startling difference in his language at the close of the book is sufficient indication of a profound change in his attitude.

A more awkward question is raised by the prosecutor, who

---

[1] p. 133. 'For the first time, the first, I laid my heart open to the benign indifference of the universe.'

[2] Philip Thody, *Albert Camus* 1913–60, p. 37.

accuses Meursault of being ignorant of the most elementary rules of human society, and of the most ordinary workings of the human heart. The reader may be forgiven if he sometimes finds himself in agreement with the prosecutor. If we accept that Camus is a moralist rather than an abstract philosopher, are we to understand that he advocates a moral attitude, or that he makes a comparative observation of moral standards? If the former, can we really suppose that he suggests we should emulate Meursault's behaviour? Is it morally admirable to murder an Arab 'because of the sun' and to show not the slightest concern for what one has done? The fate of the murdered man does not trouble Meursault; he hardly gives him a thought. We are not told whether the Arab loved life: it is unimportant. Meursault is scrupulously honest, but that is all. Honesty is not enough to make a man admirable, especially if he lacks other qualities which enrich human life. Because Camus has painted his character in such stark colours, and made of him a symbol, he risks perhaps losing the reader's sympathy, and thereby weakening the otherwise strong moral of the tale. It is unfortunate that we occasionally find our sympathies veering towards other characters who are frightened by Meursault's apparent emptiness.

Conor Cruise O'Brien has recently put forward the provocative interpretation of Meursault as a blinkered colonialist, who regards Arabs as sub-human. This may well be true, but the searing irrelevance of the point could only be missed by one who views the world through permanently fixed political spectacles. Camus does not actually tell the reader what Meursault's political attitude towards the Arabs involves. I doubt whether Meursault would have an opinion one way or the other. But O'Brien notices that the Arab does not have a name, and from this fact makes the questionable deduction that Meursault (and by extension Camus) regarded the man as not quite a man: '. . . the reader does not quite feel that Meursault has killed a man. He has killed an Arab.'[1] That some of the Europeans in the story have names, and the Arab

[1] Conor Cruise O'Brien, *Camus*, p. 25.

victim does not, means something quite different. It is surely very important to the story that the victim should be totally unknown to Meursault. If he had killed someone known to him, the novel would have taken a different turn. The question of motive would have had to be raised. Whereas, in Camus's story, it is essential that the murder be motiveless, to emphasize Meursault's status as an 'outsider' *vis-à-vis* the rest of us, who act with intention and design. He does not know the man's name because he has never met him; that is all.

The magistrate and the lawyers are also nameless. Would O'Brien suggest that *they* are 'less than human' in Camus's eyes?

Of far more interest is Robert Champigny's fascinating thesis according to which Meursault is an epicurean hero of pagan stock, a man who seeks harmony with the natural world in opposition to the Christian, who withdraws from the world. The pagan enjoys physical contact with the world, avoids abstractions which cannot bring happiness (love, ambition, hope), adapts himself to what he has and makes the most of it. Meursault undoubtedly accords with this description, of which the reader may find a fuller account in *Sur Un Héros Païen*.

With *L'Etranger* Camus achieved an artistic expression of the highest order. The flat, impersonal style is perfectly matched to the subject-matter, the austere simplicity of the narrative effectively checks any imaginative leap the reader might be tempted to make. Adjectives are used sparingly, and though the tale is told in the first person, it achieves such total objectivity as to give the impression of an impartial account. Pierre de Boisdeffre has called Camus's writing of *L'Etranger* 'un art presque invisible', and yet it hides a meticulous attention to detail. For the first time, Camus was revealed as an artist in the pure tradition of French classicism.

3

Le Mythe de Sisyphe

Only a few months after *L'Etranger* had appeared, Camus published *Le Mythe de Sisyphe*. Their close juxtaposition was appropriate, for the latter may be regarded as a commentary on the former, and for this reason it enjoyed the same immediate success. Whereas *L'Etranger* was an imaginative account of a state of mind, culminating in the discovery of a new attitude towards life, *Le Mythe de Sisyphe* is an intellectual examination of this attitude, and the state of mind which it is meant to dispel. *L'Etranger* was the story of a feeling; *Le Mythe* is the description of that feeling. It is an essay on the question which every thinking person must ask at some stage: is life really worth living? As Meursault decided in his last hours that it was, now Camus explains why he made that decision. It is an attempt to show how and why life is precious, in spite of the fact that it is pointless, meaningless, and must end in death, it is 'the soliloquy of an artist facing the idea of death'.[1] In this book there occurs for the first time the idea of the Absurd, with which Camus was henceforth to be identified.

The notion of the absurdity of the human condition was not entirely new in 1942. Sartre was busy constructing a whole ontological theory on his feeling of the contingency of existence, and French readers were already acquainted with his Roquentin, in *La Nausée*, whose reflections on man's place in a gratuitous world provided one of the great pre-war best-sellers. Malraux, too, had familiarized French readers with the concept of absurdity in human life, not to mention foreign writers the ripples of whose influence were felt in France.

[1] Conor Cruise O'Brien, op. cit., p. 30.

Camus's originality was to devote an entire book to the discussion of this feeling, and especially to make it accessible to a lay-reader by avoiding abstract philosophical theory.

The essay begins in typical block-busting, no-nonsense fashion. There is only one real problem worth considering, says Camus, and that is suicide. To decide whether or not life is worth living, is to tackle the essential question which must precede all others. Philosophical or metaphysical games for the most part elude this fundamental question.

The question once posed, you realize first of all that your life is dominated by a ludicrous obedience towards habit, and is characterized by a derisory system of mechanical gestures. You ask yourself why, and the absence of reply leaves you cold with fear. There are few moments more frightening than the sudden realization that there is no profound reason for living. When this moment happens, the walls which have so far protected you from this awful truth suddenly crumble:

> Il arrive que les décors s'écroulent. Lever, tramway, quatre heures de bureau ou d'usine, repas, tramway, quatre heures de travail, repas sommeil et lundi mardi mercredi jeudi vendredi et samedi sur le même rythme, cette route se suit aisément la plupart du temps. Un jour seulement le 'pourquoi' s'élève et tout commence dans cette lassitude teintée d'étonnement. 'Commence', ceci est important. La lassitude est à la fin des actes d'une vie machinale, mais elle inaugure en même temps le mouvement de la conscience. Elle l'éveille et elle provoque la suite. La suite, c'est le retour inconscient dans la chaine, ou c'est l'éveil définitif. . . . Le simple 'souci' est à l'origine de tout.[1]

[1] p. 27. 'It happens that the stage-sets collapse. Rising, tram, four hours in the office or the factory, meal, tram, four hours of work, meal, sleep, and Monday, Tuesday, Wednesday, Thursday, Friday and Saturday, according to the same rhythm – this path is easily followed most of the time. But one day the "why" arises and everything begins in that weariness tinged with amazement. "Begins" – this is important. Weariness comes at the end of the acts of a mechanical life, but at the same time it inaugurates the impulse of consciousness. It awakens consciousness and provokes what follows. What follows is the gradual return into the chain or it is the definitive awakening. Mere anxiety is at the source of everything.'

Most people have experienced at some time or other the sense of weariness with the pantomime which Camus describes, and many find the shock so unnerving that they close their eyes to it, and sink back into the routine which will end in death. *Le Mythe de Sisyphe* is the story of Camus's own personal refusal to sink back, and his effort to keep alive that moment of awareness, however painful it may initially be, a moment which may come as you cross the road, or as you observe a man whom you cannot hear in a telephone kiosk (p. 29).

With the moment of awareness comes a sense of exile, a feeling of being a 'stranger' in a world suddenly deprived of its familiar sense, and among people who still accept that sense. It is a lonely path that you follow if you raise disquieting questions when no one else does. (Meursault, at first, was a 'stranger' without the moment of awareness which would enable him to understand why. In spite of the first-person narrative, he is described from the outside.)

With renewed urgency, the 'aware' man turns to whatever source might offer him a reason for living, without demanding that he renegue his new-found clairvoyance.

Nature, though a source of enjoyment, serves only to emphasize his vulnerability and to reject, in its superb indifference, his search for meaning:

> Au fond de toute beauté gît quelque chose d'inhumain, et ces collines, la douceur du ciel, ces dessins d'arbres, voici qu'à la minute même, ils perdent le sens illusoire dont nous les revêtions, désormais plus lointains qu'un paradis perdu. L'hostilité primitive du monde, à travers les millénaires, remonte vers nous.[1]

Even as early as *L'Envers et L'Endroit* and *Noces*, when Camus was celebrating the pagan pleasure of tactile communion with Nature, he entertained no illusions that the natural world

[1] p. 28. 'At the heart of all beauty lies something inhuman, and these hills, the softness of the sky, the outline of these trees at this very minute lose the illusory meaning with which we had clothed them, henceforth more remote than a lost paradise. The primitive hostility of the world rises up to face us across millennia.'

might provide an answer to the problem of life. He spoke about 'L'indifférence secrète d'un des plus beaux paysages du monde', but significantly asserted that he found therein the strength to remain lucid.[1]

Nor will it help to seek a rational explanation of the world. Man's reason is inadequate to the task. With all man's equipment for rational investigation and logical analysis, he has failed miserably to establish a reason for living or to reveal an intelligible concept which explains the world beyond doubt. The scientists talk of atoms and electrons and of a physical world which obeys laws and fits a pattern, all of which sounds convincing and reassuring until one is asked to accept the end-product of scientific research, which postulates an infinity of matter revolving around an invisible nucleus. These are concepts which belong more to the realm of imaginative fantasy than to solid rational fact. The world remains obstinately irrational, irreducible:

> la raison aveugle a beau prétendre que tout est clair, j'attendais des preuves et je souhaitais qu'elle eût raison. Mais malgré tant de siècles prétentieux et par-dessus tant d'hommes éloquents et persuasifs, je sais que cela est faux.[2]

Camus has no patience with thinkers who find an explanation for the world which is beyond the scope of human reason to comprehend. He cites Chestov and Kierkegaard[3] in this regard who seem satisfied with the incomprehensibility of the world, or else identify it with God.

[1] *L'Envers et L'Endroit*, p. 94.

[2] p. 36. 'Blind reason may well claim that all is clear. I was waiting for proof and longing for it to be right. But, despite so many pretentious centuries and over the heads of so many eloquent and persuasive men, I know that is false.'

[3] Lev Shestov (1866–1939), Russian philosopher and essayist. His works include *The Apotheosis of Groundlessness* (1905), and critical books on Tolstoy, Nietzsche, and Dostoievsky. Soren Kierkegaard (1813–55). Commonly regarded as the founder of modern Existentialism, Kierkegaard was born in Copenhagen, where he became a distinguished theologian. His system was based on the antipathy between thought and existence.

Car lorsqu'au terme de ses analyses passionées Chestov découvre l'absurdité fondamentale de toute existence, il ne dit point: 'Voici l'absurde', mais 'Voici Dieu' . . . Pour Chestov, la raison est vaine, mais il y a quelque chose au-delà de la raison. Pour un esprit absurde, la raison est vaine et il n'y a rien au-delà de la raison.[1]

Camus says quite bluntly that reason is all we possess to understand the world and our place within it, yet reason is quite inefficient – it will not provide us with an answer. We must be honest and recognize the limitations of human reason, at the same time refusing to admit that which we are incapable of understanding. (To do so would be an ontological nonsense.)

Having recognized that the human presence carries no specific rational justification, the fact remains that man's desire that it should is no less strong. It is this eternal disparity between man's need for coherence and order, and the world's stubborn disorder and incoherence, which constitutes the absurd. 'Ce divorce entre l'homme et de sa vie, l'acteur et son décor, c'est proprement le sentiment de l'absurdité.'[2] On the one hand, there is a world which is unintelligible, on the other a human presence which passionately desires intelligibility; the two run on parallel lines, but never meet in a consummate understanding. Camus called one of his plays '*Le Malentendu*'; in it, Martha says, 'il y a eu malentendu. Et pour peu que vous connaissiez le monde, vous ne vous en étonnerez pas.'[3] It is essential to Camus's thesis that there will always be this 'misunderstanding' between man and his world; the world will always resist analysis, man will always want to analyse. His demand for coherence is therefore destined to be forever frustrated.

[1] pp. 53, 55. 'For when, at the conclusion of his passionate analyses, Chestov discovers the fundamental absurdity of all existence, he does not say: "This is the absurd", but rather "This is God." To Chestov reason is useless but there is something beyond reason. To an absurd mind reason is useless and there is nothing beyond reason.'

[2] p. 18. 'This divorce between man and his life, the actor and his setting, is properly the feeling of absurdity.'

[3] p. 97. 'There has been a misunderstanding. And if only you knew the world, you would not be so surprised.' (BM)

It now becomes clear that it would be seriously to misunderstand Camus to say that he regards the world as absurd, or to say that he regards man as absurd. What is absurd is the *relationship* between man and the objects of his understanding, the link which ties man to the world. The world is not absurd, it is irrational, incongruous. The Absurd is born of man's dissatisfaction with this irrationality:

> Ce monde en lui-même n'est pas raisonnable, c'est tout ce qu'on en peut dire. Mais ce qui est absurde, c'est la confrontation de cet irrationnel et de ce désir éperdu de clarté dont l'appel résonne au plus profond de l'homme. L'absurde dépend autant de l'homme que du monde. Il est pour le moment leur seul lien. (p. 37) . . . l'homme se trouve devant l'irrationnel. Il sent en lui son désir de bonheur et de raison. L'absurde naît de cette confrontation entre l'appel humain et le silence déraisonnable du monde. . . . L'irrationnel, la nostalgie humaine et l'absurde qui surgit de leur tête-à-tête . . .[1]

It follows that man is the most essential element in this trinity, for without his refusal to accept the world's incongruity, the Absurd would not reveal itself. As long as man remains aware, without illusion and without escape, that the world is inexplicable, and maintains at the same time a constant need to explain, his questions will echo hollow in the Absurd. 'L'absurde est essentiellement un divorce. Il n'est ni dans l'un ni dans l'autre des éléments comparés. Il naît de leur confrontation.'[2] If we were to accept the irrationality of the universe and the senselessness of human existence (and most of us do most of the time),

---

[1] pp. 37, 44–5. 'This world in itself is not reasonable, that is all that can be said. But what is absurd is the confontration of the irrational and the wild longing for clarity whose call echoes in the human heart. The absurd depends as much on man as on the world. For the moment it is all that links them together . . . man stands face to face with the irrational. He feels within him his longing for happiness and for reason. The absurd is born of this confrontation between the human need and the unreasonable silence of the world. . . . The irrational, the human nostalgia, and the absurd that is born of their encounter.'

[2] p. 48. 'The absurd is essentially a divorce. It lies in neither of the elements compared; it is born of their confrontation.'

then there is no question of absurdity, because there is no confrontation, no disparity between our desires and their impossibility of satisfaction. But this attitude is no longer possible after a moment of awareness, similar to that experienced by Meursault on the last page of *L'Etranger*. One must *object* to the human condition for it to be rendered absurd. 'L'absurde n'a de sens que dans la mesure où l'on n'y consent pas.'[1]

If I have dealt at some length with the precise definition of Camus's concept of the Absurd, it is because it is the starting-point of his whole attitude towards life. It means that the decks are swept completely clean, that truth is relative, that chance governs the world, that the conflict between man's desperate need to exercise his understanding and the resistance that he encounters is insoluble, in short that all his efforts are vain. Above all, even if he were to achieve some coherence, it would avail him little, since he is irrevocably condemned to death.

It is as well to recall, at this point, that Albert Camus came close to death on more than one occasion. His tuberculosis was a sinister reminder of the mortal condition which makes nonsense of all our aspirations. The fact of death is a simple one, and no one would pretend that he is not subject to it. For the most part, however, we lead lives in such a way that we might seem entirely ignorant of the final act, the ultimate absurdity that is played upon us. Were Camus a healthier man, I doubt whether he would have reflected upon the fact of death with such intensity, and his work might have taken a different turn. As it is, his hospitalization made this naturally contemplative man realize the full implications of human mortality, which one normally would employ every effort in concealing. For the implications are depressing almost beyond endurance. Life is useless. Man aspires towards eternity and is crushed beneath the 'bloody mathematics' of his condition:

> J'en viens enfin à la mort et au sentiment que nous en avons. Sur ce point tout a été dit et il est décent de se

---

[1] p. 50. 'The absurd has meaning only in so far as it is not agreed to.'

garder du pathétique. On ne s'étonnera cependant jamais
assez de ce que tout le monde vive comme si personne 'ne
savait' . . . Aucune morale, ni aucun effort ne sont *a
priori* justifiables devant les sanglantes mathématiques
qui ordonnent notre condition.[1]

The view which Camus gives of the human condition is, thus
far, horribly black. One might be forgiven for regarding such a
view as pessimistic, were it to stop there. But the originality
and the grandeur of Camus lie in his ability to wrench a positive
attitude from such negative premises. He goes to the very
brink of nihilism, in full consciousness of the truth which leads
there, yet emerges with an alternative reaction which is valid.
First, he considers various responses to a recognition of the
Absurd: despair, suicide, and hope.

Despair is the most obvious response. Like Alceste (in
Molière's *Misanthrope*), one could retire to a little black corner
and berate the injustice of one's lot. Despair is too bleak and
sterile for Camus. Some years later, in his *Lettres à un Ami
Allemand*, he stated categorically that 'vous acceptiez légère-
ment de désespérer et que je n'y ai jamais consenti'.[2]

A more dramatic response is suicide. Certainly it would seem
the most logical action to take. If life has no sense, then it does
not matter, in any real way, whether I live or die, and since I
know that there never will be any sense, no matter how much
I may yearn for it, I might as well advance the day of a death
which is anyway inevitable: it is only a matter of timing. Camus
understands and to a certain extent sympathizes with this
feeling.

Soudain il découvre ceci que demain sera semblable,
et après-demain, tous les autres jours. Et cette irrémédi-
able découverte l'écrase. Ce sont de pareilles idées qui

---

[1] pp. 29–30. 'I come at last to death and to the attitude we have towards
it. On this point everything has been said and it is only proper to avoid
pathos. Yet one will never be sufficiently surprised that everyone lives as
if no one "knew". . . . No code of ethics and no effort are justifiable *a
priori* in the face of the cruel mathematics that command our condition.'
[2] p. 72. 'You calmly accepted despair and I have always refused it.' (BM)

vous font mourir. Pour ne pouvoir les supporter, on se
tue – ou si l'on est jeune, on en fait des phrases.[1]

Suicide is, however, not a solution because it confirms the
Absurd, without resolving it. Since the Absurd arises, we have
seen, from an awareness of the confrontation between man's
aspirations and the impossibility that they will be fulfilled, one
cannot eliminate one of the elements of that confrontation by
annihilation of the awareness.[2] Suicide does not refute the
Absurd, it intensifies it, or surrenders to it. There is a difference
between deciding that life is meaningless and deciding that it
is not worth living; indeed, Camus's whole work is a clarification of that difference. People who kill themselves are confusing
two separate issues. They assume that it is a logical step from
the realization that existence is irrational to the determination
to put an end to it. But this is a spurious logic. One cannot de-
duce anything from the irrationality of the world except that it
is irrational. To say that, therefore, life is not worth living is a
non-sequitur. On the contrary, life is senseless, but *nevertheless*
it is worth living.

> On choisit de durer dès l'instant qu'on ne se laisse pas
> mourir et l'on reconnaît alors une valeur, au moins rela-
> tive, à la vie.[3]

The Absurd is only revealed by an effort of the conscious, but
the conscious must not connive at the Absurd by ceasing to be.
Camus here requires no mean degree of heroism on the part of
the man who has become 'aware', the sort of heroism shown by

---

[1] *L'Envers et L'Endroit*, p. 46. 'Suddenly he discovers that tomorrow
will be the same as today, and the day after, and every other day. And he is
crushed by this irrevocable discovery. It is thoughts like these that make
one die. Because you can't stand them, you kill yourself – or if you are
young, you make speeches about them.' (BM)

[2] cf. *L'Homme Révolté*, p. 16. 'The rejection of suicide and the maintenance of that hopeless confrontation between human questioning and the
silence of the world.' (BM)

[3] *Eté*, p. 148. 'The very fact that you do not let yourself die means that
you have chosen to carry on, and in so doing, you recognize that life has a
value, albeit relative.' (BM)

the man in the condemned cell. 'Le contraire du suicide, précisément, c'est le condamné à mort.'[1] The significance of Meursault's final outburst in favour of life now becomes more apparent. It is the very opposite of the acquiescence which the suicide explicitly shows. The condemned man raises his voice, at the last moment, in the face of certain death, to protest against the absurd injustice which makes life end in extinction; the suicide meets absurdity with a whimper. Camus asks the reader to make the imaginative leap from the particular to the general, and to see that we are all, in fact, in the condemned cell, under sentence of death, with the sole difference that the date of execution has not been set. If only we were to realize this, fully and consciously, we should act with the same assertive power as the prisoner whose final day has been announced, and yell our protest against the injustice of mortality. For Camus, it is inconceivable that anyone should compound that injustice by taking his own life. That would be, in effect, to take sides with the injustice of the world, to increase it, to abnegate the human role, which is a constantly vigilant awareness of the human condition.

There is a personal reason for Camus's frequent reference to the condemned cell. His mother told how his father, whom he never knew, once attended an execution in Constantine. He came home ashen-faced, shocked, and silent. It seems she told the story to Camus when he was an adolescent. The image never left him. It epitomized for him all that was horrible, inexplicable, and revolting in the world, and it crops up in his writing time and again. In *Le Mythe de Sisyphe*, the image of the condemned man serves to provide a striking contrast with the suicide, and to proclaim the incomparable freedom that total awareness of one's fate must bring. Irrelevancies are swept aside, the truth of one's position clearly perceived, perhaps for the first time:

> La divine disponibilité du condamné à mort devant qui s'ouvrent les portes de la prison par une certaine petite

aube, cet incroyable désintéressement à l'égard de tout, sauf de la flamme pure de la vie, la mort et l'absurde sont ici, on le sent bien, les principes de la seule liberté raisonnable: celle qu'un cœur humain peut éprouver et vivre.[1]

The above passage might be a commentary on the last page of *L'Etranger*.

The third response to a discovery of the Absurd is to hope that it is temporary. If the world seems at the moment to be cruel and inexplicable, let us trust that one day it will be benevolent, and susceptible to understanding. All will eventually be explained. This, put baldly, is the basic religious doctrine of faith in an unknowable future. It is a doctrine of consolation and comfort, and however effective it may be in some circumstances, it is unacceptable to Camus. There is a difference, he says, between what is true and what is desirable. Of course, man desires a tomorrow, a permanence, an eternity, but to expect that this desire will be fulfilled, when it is admittedly an unanswerable question (and therefore irrelevant to life), is a cruel evasion of his present condition, and the consequences he should draw from it. Since we have rejected suicide, what we have to deal with is how to live now. We have recognized that life has no sense or purpose, yet we have resolved to live it. We must now further recognize that we shall live *without hope*; our present state is our only state. There is no tomorrow.

Camus is emphatic in his assertion that the rejection of hope does not predicate despair or resignation. Quite the contrary. To live without hope is not to live in despair, it is to live without illusion. The religious view, on the other hand, *is* a desperate one. To live in hope for the future life is to reject the life that we have which (to Camus) would be the ultimate 'sin'. He holds that the religious position, which throws in the towel,

---

[1] p. 83. 'The divine availability of the condemned man before whom the prison doors open in a certain early dawn, that unbelievable disinterestedness with regard to everything except for the pure flame of life – it is clear that death and the absurd are here the principles of the only reasonable freedom: that which a human heart can experience and live.'

'gives up' life in favour of a postulated spiritual existence, can with more justice be called 'resignation'. The religious man is resigned to the absurdity of his existence, and seeks refuge in a wholly untenable metaphysical belief. The man who lives without hope has *accepted* his condition in the world and has resolved to live it as best he can. The religious attitude involves a suspension of activity; the 'hopeless' attitude, we shall see, is active and vigorous. A chasm separates the abnegation and resignation of the religious man from the constant and clair-voyant activity of the man who has determined to live without hope. He will find his greatest incarnation in Dr Rieux, the narrator of *La Peste*. Considerable courage is required to live without spiritual comfort. Camus is not insensitive to the fact that the temptation to give up is never far away:

> A un certain point de son chemin, l'homme absurde est sollicité. L'histoire ne manque ni de religions, ni de prophètes, même sans dieux. On lui demande de sauter. Tout ce qu'il peut répondre, c'est qu'il ne comprend pas bien, que cela n'est pas évident. Il ne veut faire justement que ce qu'il comprend bien. On lui assure que c'est péché d'orgueil, mais il n'entend pas la notion de péché; que peut-être l'enfer est au bout, mais il n'a pas assez d'imagination pour se représenter cet étrange avenir; qu'il perd la vie immortelle, mais cela lui paraît futile. On voudrait lui faire reconnaître sa culpabilité. Lui se sent innocent. . . . Ainsi ce qu'il exige de lui-même, c'est de vivre *seulement* avec ce qu'il sait, de s'arranger de ce qui est et ne rien faire intervenir qui ne soit certain. On lui répond que rien ne l'est. Mais ceci du moins est une certitude. C'est avec elle qu'il a affaire: il veut savoir s'il est possible de vivre sans appel.[1]

[1] pp. 75–6. 'At a certain point on his path the absurd man is tempted. History is not lacking in either religions or prophets, even without gods. He is asked to leap. All that he can reply is that he doesn't fully understand, that it is not obvious. Indeed, he does not want to do anything but what he fully understands. He is assured that this is the sin of pride, but he does not understand the notion of sin; that perhaps hell is in store, but he has not enough imagination to visualize that strange future; that he is losing immortal life, but that seems to him an idle consideration. An attempt is made to get him to admit his guilt. He feels innocent. . . . Hence what he

Now that despair, suicide, and metaphysical hope have all
been rejected as possible responses to the absurdity of man's
position, because they all involve either resignation or flight
from life, the only alternative which remains is to live life to the
full *in spite of* its being meaningless, all the time cherishing
one's awareness that it is meaningless. Camus calls this attitude
the position of revolt. It is a revolt which is doomed to failure,
because it is a revolt against man's mortality, but it must be
maintained in full consciousness of its inefficacy, precisely
because it is the only attitude which does not deny, stifle or
distort one's awareness. Revolt is the only *honest* attitude, the
only response to life which faces the hard facts squarely and
refuses all concealment. We are not speaking of a rebellion
which seeks to render the world rational, since it will always be
irrational; nor can it offer a meaning to life, which will always
be meaningless. We are speaking of a revolt which accepts its
limitations, knows that the absurd makes everything pointless,
but keeps alive at least the one human quality about which there
is no doubt – awareness without illusion:

> Il s'agissait précédemment de savoir si la vie devait avoir
> un sens pour être vécue. Il apparaît ici au contraire qu'elle
> sera d'autant mieux vécue qu'elle n'aura pas de sens.
> Vivre une expérience, un destin, c'est l'accepter pleine-
> ment. . . . L'une des seules positions philosophiques
> cohérentes, c'est ainsi la révolte. Elle est un confrontement
> perpétuel de l'homme et de sa propre obscurité.[1] Elle
> n'est pas aspiration, elle est sans espoir. Cette révolte

---

demands of himself is to live *solely* with what he knows, to accommodate
himself to what is and to bring in nothing that is not certain. He is told
that nothing is. But that at least is a certainty. And it is with this that he is
concerned: he wants to find out if it is possible to live without appeal.'

[1] p. 76. 'It was previously a question of finding out whether or not life
had to have a meaning to be lived. It now becomes clear on the contrary
that it will be lived all the better if it has no meaning. Living an experience,
a particular fate, is accepting it fully. . . . One of the only coherent philosophical positions is thus revolt. It is a constant confrontation between man
and his own obscurity.'

n'est que l'assurance d'un destin écrasant, moins la résignation qui devrait l'accompagner.[1]

The spectacle of a defiance which accepts the immutability of that which it defies might seem at best fruitless. It is a paradox, and, it must be admitted, a muddle-headed exercise in philosophical thinking. In strictly philosophical terms, Camus's revolt is total paralysis, leading nowhere, least of all to the kind of positive, constructive life which he advocates. I said at the beginning, however, that Camus was not a philosopher; it is unfair, then, to be disappointed in his performance. If we examine his thinking rather more closely, we see that his revolt promotes specifically human qualities of justice and happiness (qualities for which there has been no logical preparation) to counteract the irrationality of life. In *Lettres à un Ami Allemand* he writes, 'l'homme devait affirmer la justice pour lutter contre l'injustice éternelle, créer du bonheur pour protester contre l'univers du malheur'.[2] Camus is not advocating a philosophy, so much as a humanist ethic, which is not *philosophically* justified by what has gone before, but is *emotionally* justified. *Le Mythe de Sisyphe* is more an urgent emotional plea than a cerebral investigation. Camus wants his revolt to restore to men the dignity and honour which he feels the absurdity of human existence denies them. '. . . refusant d'admettre ce désespoir et ce monde torturé, je voulais seulement que les hommes retrouvent leur solidarité pour entrer en lutte contre leur destin révoltant.'[3] Camus's heart is warmed by the spectacle of men struggling hopelessly against an unjust fate. He was to devote his finest book, *La Peste*, to a celebration of this image of Men in Revolt.

[1] p. 77. 'It is not aspiration, for it is devoid of hope. That revolt is the certainty of a crushing fate, without the resignation that ought to accompany it.'

[2] p. 72. 'Man should proclaim justice in order to fight against eternal injustice, he should create happiness as a protest against the world of unhappiness.' (BM)

[3] ibid., p. 73. 'refusing to allow this despair and this tormented world, I wanted only that men should rediscover their solidarity so as to wage war against their disgusting fate.' (BM)

It is essential to remember that *lucidity* is the most important element in this revolt. Camus means by this word both a clear-sighted view of the human dilemma, and an inviolable honesty which must result from this view. We must have the lucidity to keep before us a constantly sharp awareness that life is meaningless, we must not falter in our contemplation of the Absurd, and we must have the honesty to admit that this *is* the human condition, that it cannot be mitigated, that it is cruel, hideous, stupid. Any attempt to cover the truth, we must resist. In *L'Envers et L'Endroit* Camus wrote, 'Et j'ai besoin de ma lucidité. Oui, tout est simple, Ce sont les hommes qui compliquent les choses. Qu'on ne nous raconte pas d'histoires. Qu'on ne nous dise pas du condamné à mort: "Il va payer sa dette à la société", mais: "On va lui couper le cou." Ça n'a l'air de rien. Mais ça fait une petite différence. Et puis, il y a des gens qui préfèrent regarder leur destin dans les yeux.'[1] The same attitude was to be echoed by Dr Rieux, in *La Peste*, who said that the question was to decide whether or not two and two made four, and, if they did, to admit as much, and to act accordingly (*La Peste*, p. 150). Camus himself is lucid and honest enough to be loyal to his human state, and not mask the truth beneath a supernatural or philosophical abstraction. Once again, however, the concept of honesty has crept into the argument almost unawares, without preparation and without any ontological justification. There is nothing, logically, to prevent one from being lucidly aware of the irrationality of the world and the absurdity of man's demands upon it, yet to be dishonest about the consequences of these thoughts. The fact that I do not *lie* about what I discern to be true is not because I have no alternative, but because I make a value judgement and decide I *should* tell the truth. I should, because man is worthy of honesty and dignity. If I were to believe that

[1] 'My lucidity is necessary to me. Yes, it is all very simple – only men complicate matters. Don't let them spin you any yarns. Don't let them tell you that the man condemned to death "is going to pay his debt towards society", but rather "his neck is going to be broken". It doesn't seem much; but it makes a little difference. Besides, there are people who prefer to look their fate in the eyes.' (BM)

mankind was not worth fighting for, even talking about and writing about, Camus's arguments would hold no conviction for me. Underlying *Le Mythe de Sisyphe* is a fundamental, impregnable belief in the value of man which is not thought out, but instinctively felt. 'J'exalte l'homme devant ce qui l'écrase.'[1]

Revolt reveals a new and profound freedom. Before the moment of awareness overwhelms us, we prize a liberty which is illusory. Camus lists the familiar ways in which this freedom is expressed. We are free to have aims and purposes in life, to plan for our retirement or the future of our children, to act in accordance with design and ambition. Camus says that this freedom is a delusion because, in the end, we are not free to perpetuate our existence. 'La mort est là comme seule réalité.'[2] In a way, we are enslaved to this freedom, for our actions must conform with whatever aim we have set for ourselves, in order to realize it (pp. 80–1). Genuine freedom arises once we have recognized the fatuity of all human ambition. 'L'absurde m'éclaire sur ce point: il n'y a pas de lendemain. Voici désormais la raison de ma liberté profonde.'[3] We are free, in other words, because we are aware of our mortality. There is a semantic confusion here between two varieties of 'freedom'. As Dr Cruickshank has convincingly shown,[4] the freedom which precedes awareness is freedom from restraint, the capacity to act without fear of prevention, whereas the freedom Camus talks of after the moment of awareness is of a different order: it is a freedom of the mind, 'consciousness of necessity'. The new freedom consists in the knowledge that we are *not* free from restraint, since death is the ultimate check. It is a paradox which Camus does not examine.

If revolt rejects the future, it embraces the present with passion. Once ambitions and projects have been dismissed, the

---

[1] p. 119. 'I exalt man before what crushes him.'

[2] 'Death is there as the only reality.'

[3] p. 82. 'The absurd enlightens me on this point: there is no future. Henceforth this is the reason for my inner freedom.'

[4] John Cruickshank, op. cit., pp. 71–2.

present moment becomes the moment to live for. 'Si je refuse obstinément tous les "plus tard" du monde, c'est qu'il s'agit aussi bien de ne pas renoncer à ma richesse présente',[1] wrote Camus in *Noces*. The same notion is to be found in *L'Etranger*. Camus now explains that the 'aware' man rejoices in each successive present moment as part of his revolt against a meaningless and finite existence. Revolt commands an ethic of quantity rather than quality. 'Ce qui compte n'est pas de vivre le mieux mais de vivre le plus.'[2] 'Quality' is suggested by abstract concepts which exist outside time. Now that all abstract concepts have been overthrown and the finite power of time recognized, quantity is more important, because one can no longer believe that any experience is qualitatively more profound than any other. 'Le présent et la succession des présents devant une âme sans cesse consciente, c'est l'idéal de l'homme absurde.'[3] Camus intends this notion to convey an intense commitment to life as it is, and as such it is attractive. His own life is a fine illustration of this 'free' ethic. It is a pity that in *Le Mythe de Sisyphe* it sometimes sounds like selfish hedonism. The trouble is that this essay is in many ways a selfish book, in the sense that Camus here explains his *own* path in coming to terms with life. In *La Peste* the ethic will expand to embrace his attitude towards other people when we shall see that the notion of quantity is restricted by a higher value of solidarity with all who suffer from injustice.

In replacing quality by quantity, the 'aware' man effectively rids himself of any need to look for meaning and significance. 'Ne pas croire au sens profond des choses, c'est le propre de l'homme absurde.'[4] Instead of looking for meaning, he embraces life, with the implication that if he did not love life, it

---

[1] p. 27. 'If I reject all the "wait and sees" of this world, it is as much so as not to renounce my present richness.' (BM)

[2] p. 84. 'What counts is not the best living but the most living.'

[3] p. 88. 'The present and the succession of presents before a constantly conscious soul is the ideal of the absurd man.'

[4] p. 100. 'Not to believe in the profound meaning of things belongs to the absurd man.'

would avail him little to know what life meant. He reasserts priorities; *how* one lives and the *degree* to which one lives are more important than *why* one lives. Camus's most acute anxiety is that we should admit the startling simplicity of all essential matters, once the entanglements of scientific interpretation, mystical significance, philosophical complications, have been disposed of. Life is to be lived, because it is all we have, and it is to be lived in the full knowledge that it is finite and senseless. 'Ainsi, chaque fois qu'il m'a semblé éprouver le sens profond du monde, c'est sa simplicité qui m'a toujours bouleversé.'[1]

It is now possible to form a clear picture of what Camus calls *l'homme absurde*, and what I have called, to avoid an ambiguous translation, the 'aware' man. He is a man who knows his destiny but rebels against it, has no regrets for the past or hope for the future, whose freedom from illusion commits him passionately to life in the present. He rejects both suicide and the leap of faith, values the dignity of man and honesty, speaks with remorseless clarity to dispel the fog of deceit which enshrouds the ineluctable fact of his mortality. (In later books, he promotes justice in order to alleviate the natural injustice of his condition.) Camus offers four illustrations of such a life: the lover, the actor, the adventurer and the man of letters.

The lover is represented by Don Juan, in whom the ethic of quantity is most clearly apparent. Don Juan opts for plurality of experience, he maximizes present pleasures, considers remorse a vain emotion, and the concepts of salvation and damnation empty ideas. He replaces concepts by sensations and, like Meursault in *L'Etranger*, recognizes only the sensual life.

The actor is likewise firmly committed to the present, and to a multiplicity of experience, which changes with every role he assumes. He gives equal intensity to each role, in spite of the

---

[1] *L'Envers et L'Endroit*, p. 66. 'So, every time that I seemed to feel the profound meaning of the world, it was its simplicity which always overwhelmed me.' (BM)

clear knowledge that the personality he represents is finite. Death comes to him at the end of every performance. He is a man with a zest for life, for each life he plays, and he entertains no delusions about its significance.

Thirdly, the adventurer is evidently married to the present and to the quantitative ethic. He rebels against his mortal condition by a constantly active existence.

The creative artist is the fourth example of a clairvoyant existence, for the writer multiplies his life of thought and feeling by reflecting it in his art. 'Créer, c'est vivre deux fois.'[1] At the same time, he knows that his work carries no more inherent significance than the succession of experiences in which the actor and the lover indulge. Like them, he is free from illusion. Writing does not resolve man's dilemma, it describes it (p. 129). It must not attempt to offer a rational explanation of life, but to present the unadorned truth. In its clairvoyance, it therefore exemplifies the position of revolt. The writer fixes the world in his sights and protests against it, knowing that his protest is doomed to impotence. Nothing can alter the fact of the Absurd; the writer's function resides in capturing and proclaiming it.

Each of these examples of the 'aware' man is conscious of the utter futility of his activity. The finest embodiment of Camus's vision is taken from mythology and lends his name to the title of the essay. It is Sisyphus who, after an existence of sensual enjoyment, in which he dismissed the gods, was condemned by them to push a rock to the top of a hill in perpetuity. Each time he reached the summit, the rock would roll down again, and his task would be renewed. Sisyphus is tragic, but he is superior to his fate, because he is conscious of it. With total lucidity, he is aware that his task is useless and destined always to be thwarted. He faces his torment and will not be dominated by it:

> Si ce mythe est tragique, c'est que son héros est conscient. Où serait en effet sa peine, si à chaque pas l'espoir de réussir le soutenait ? L'ouvrier d'aujourd'hui travaille, tous

[1] p. 128. 'Creating is living doubly.'

les jours de sa vie, aux mêmes tâches et ce destin n'est pas moins absurde. Mais il n'est tragique qu'aux rares moments où il devient conscient. Sisyphe, prolétaire des dieux, impuissant et révolté, connaît toute l'étendue de sa misérable condition: c'est à elle qu'il pense pendant sa descente. La clairvoyance qui devait faire son tourment consomme du même coup sa victoire. Il n'est pas de destin qui ne se surmonte par le mépris.[1]

Camus's contention is that, like Sisyphus, we can dominate the horrid facts of the human dilemma by facing them. Our power of awareness is our trump card. As Sisyphus struggles with his heavy weight up the never-ending slope, so we must struggle with the senselessness of our condition in full consciousness that it will never be alleviated. It is a stern, stoical message that Camus brings in his essay, but one which he believes can lead to a modicum of happiness, derived from an obstinate lucidity, and a tenacious display of dignity. Sisyphus does not despair. His struggle brings its own reward:

La lutte elle-même vers les sommets suffit à remplir un cœur d'homme. Il faut imaginer Sisyphe heureux.[2]

*   *   *

Le Malentendu and Caligula

In 1944, Camus's first two plays were produced, *Le Malentendu* and *Caligula*. Both illustrate themes taken from *Le Mythe de Sisyphe*.

In *Le Malentendu* Martha and her mother are proprietors

[1] pp. 163–4. 'If this myth is tragic, that is because its hero is conscious. Where would his torture be, indeed, if at every step the hope of succeeding upheld him? The workman of today works every day in his life at the same tasks and his fate is no less absurd. But it is tragic only at the rare moments when it becomes conscious. Sisyphus, proletarian of the gods, powerless and rebellious, knows the whole extent of his wretched condition; it is what he thinks of during his descent. The lucidity that was to constitute torture at the same time crowns his victory. There is no fate that cannot be surmounted by scorn.'

[2] p. 166. 'The struggle itself towards the heights is enough to fill a man's heart. One must imagine Sisyphus happy.'

of a country inn. They rob and murder any wealthy guests who come their way. One day, a stranger arrives and asks for a room. It is Martha's brother Jan, who has returned after an absence of twenty years to take his mother and sister to the land of sunshine for which they yearn. But he makes the fatal mistake of not announcing his identity. He is not recognized, is murdered, and dumped in the river. The following day his wife Maria arrives, and reveals the awful truth. Martha hangs herself, and her mother drowns in the river.

This is a profoundly pessimistic play set in a world of bitter irony. The 'misunderstanding' of the title represents both the non-recognition of the son by mother and sister (based on a legendary story which crops up in folklore), and also the lack of comprehension between man and the world. 'Ce monde lui-même n'est pas raisonnable,' says the mother, 'et je puis bien le dire, moi qui en ai tout goûté, depuis la création jusqu'à la destruction.'[1] It is a depressing picture of malevolent fate, which thwarts every human desire or intention. The irony of the play is overwhelming. Jan comes to bring happiness to his mother and sister, he accepts his responsibility as a 'life' person, he wants to do his duty; instead, he brings murder to himself, despair and suicide to his family. The mother wants rest and peace; she gets heartache, remorse, and death. Martha wants happiness, the sun, freedom; she gets bitterness and death. Maria claims simple personal happiness, and her life is ruined. All but Maria are the unwitting authors of their own destruction. Their efforts achieve the opposite of their intentions and bring disaster. Such is the order of the world, implies Camus, where human desires count for nothing in the irrational cosmos, where no one is 'recognized'.

There is something wrong with this beautifully-constructed irony. If *Le Malentendu* is intended as an allegory of the injustice of the world, then the calamitous events should not be brought about by human agency. If only Jan had identified himself, all would have been well. It is difficult to see how an

---

[1] p. 86. 'This world itself is not rational, I can tell you, I who have tasted all of life, from creating it to destroying it.' (BM)

irrational cosmos can be blamed for human whimsy. The allegorical power of the play is diluted by this error in conception.

Martha is presumably the heroine of the piece. She incarnates many of the characteristics of the 'aware' man described in *Le Mythe de Sisyphe*, She refuses to tell lies. 'Je n'aime pas les allusions,'[1] she says, and 'J'ai toujours trouvé de l'avantage à montrer les choses telles qu'elles sont.'[2] She is dupe to no illusion. She says that she 'hates' God, who is represented by the ambiguous old man in the last scene with one word to say, the last of the play, 'Non'. She is the only character in the whole of Camus's work to use the word hate; it is untypical of his vocabulary and his attitudes. Where Martha divorces herself even more from Camus's ideal is, of course, in her suicide. The truly 'aware' man does not surrender to the Absurd.

Le Malentendu is a grotesque picture of the lack of communication between people, not between people and the world. Camus himself said in conversation that his play was a plea for simple sincerity.[3]

Caligula takes an historical subject and treats it, again, as an allegory of the Absurd. At the death of his sister and mistress, Drusilla, Caligula is suddenly aware, for the first time, of the simple truth that men die and are not happy. He resolves to make men face this truth, recognize the absurdity and injustice of life, and thereby dominate it. How? By a reign of arbitrary terror which will proclaim the Absurd loudly, and force men to be aware of it. The Patricians are rebellious, but Cherea advises them to allow Caligula's madness to play itself out. Caligula piles crime upon crime until he is eventually murdered by the conspirators.

Caligula is the tragedy of a sensitive man who does the wrong things for the right reasons. At the beginning of the play, he is grief-stricken by the death of his sister and disgusted with a

[1] p. 17. 'I don't like allusions.'
[2] p. 42. 'I have always found it better to show things exactly as they are.' (BM)
[3] *Pléiade*, p. 1729.

creation which allows death to occur so arbitrarily and so soon:

> Ce monde, tel qu'il est fait, n'est pas supportable. J'ai
> donc besoin de la lune, ou du bonheur, ou de l'immortalité,
> de quelque chose qui soit dément peut-être, mais qui ne
> soit pas de ce monde.[1]

So far, he expresses a feeling which is perfectly understandable,
the longing for a 'better life' which is the basis of all religious
temptation. But an excess of zeal drives him to make his subjects share his new 'awareness' of their misery. He proposes to
shake them from their complacency:

> Alors, c'est que tout, autour de moi, est mensonge, et moi,
> je veux qu'on vive dans la vérité! Et justement, j'ai les
> moyens de les faire vivre dans la vérité. Car je sais ce
> qui leur manque, Hélicon. Ils sont privés de la connais-
> sance et il leur manque un professeur qui sache ce dont
> il parle.[2]

His motives, then, are of the best, but his methods prove to
be disastrous. With ruthless logic, he pursues the consequences
of his discovery to their extreme limit. He kills for no reason,
rapes a woman in front of her husband, closes the wheat
market and declares an artificial and unnecessary famine,
forces his victims to smile in their suffering. He challenges the
values of the Patricians, their belief in reason, their assumpton
that there is an order in the world, by the systematic destruction of their security and their values, the institution of a rule
of capricious cruelty. He says that he thinks all values are equal;
there is no difference in quality, therefore, between the famine
that he has declared and his satiety at meals. Caligula knows
that death renders all useless, so why pretend there is a differ-

[1] p. 121. 'This world is not tolerable as it is. I need the moon, or some
happiness, or immortality, something lunatic perhaps, but something which
is not of this world.' (BM)

[2] p. 122. 'Everything around me is lies and deceit. I want people to live
in the truth. And I have the means to make them live in the truth. For I
know what they are lacking, Hélicon. They are deprived of knowledge and
they lack a teacher who knows what he is talking about.' (BM)

ence. And since death cannot be avoided, it does not really matter if he advances the day by a few years. This is the logic of the Absurd, the consequence of facing the truth at all times, 'cette logique implacable qui broie les vies humaines'.[1]

What Caligula has done is to become God. 'J'ai simplement compris qu'il n'y a qu'une façon de s'égaler aux dieux: il suffit d'être aussi cruel qu'eux,'[2] he says. And again, 'il est permis à tout homme de jouer les tragédies célestes et de devenir dieu. Il suffit de se durcir le cœur.'[3] In his misguided crusade, the erstwhile gentle emperor has taken it upon himself to become as insensitive a tyrant as the gods (or God, or Fate) whom he detests. It is understood that this is not a procedure of which Camus approves. As Martha in *Le Malentendu* succumbed to the Absurd by killing herself, so Caligula surrenders to the Absurd by playing its game. His furious and capricious tyranny merely intensifies the Absurd by compounding the injustice of the world. Caesonia says to him, 'Mais si le mal est sur la terre, pourquoi y ajouter?'[4]

There is in the play, however, an *homme absurde* who is just as lucid as Caligula, who has no illusions, who also fights against the intolerable pointlessness of life, but who is saved from the nihilistic spiral down which Caligula descends by compassion for the miserable state of men. This is Cherea. For him, truth must take second place to happiness. He knows that his is a pragmatic and limited view, and that logically Caligula is right, but he holds out for a little happiness, without relaxing his rebellion against unhappiness. Cherea remains a man among men, while Caligula has allowed his enthusiasm to sweep aside his natural humanity. Cherea is the forerunner of Dr Rieux (in *La Peste*) and the first of Camus's creations to

---

[1] p. 247. 'This implacable logic which crushes human lives.' (BM)

[2] p. 192. 'I have simply understood that there is only one way to make oneself equal to the gods: you must be as cruel as they are.' (BM)

[3] p. 196. 'Anyone can play the celestial game and become god. You have only to harden your heart.' (BM)

[4] p. 136. 'But if evil is on the world, why seek to add to it?' (BM)

show altruism. He looks outwards, not inwards like Meursault or the hypothetical embodiment of Sisyphus.

*   *   *

In 1944, Albert Camus was the author of a revolutionary new novel, an introspective essay, two collections of short stories and essays, and two plays. His employment was as a reader for the publishing house Gallimard. Then, on 24 August 1944 there appeared the first open issue of *Combat*, with the name of Camus as its editor. *Combat* had until then been a clandestine source of information disseminated by the Resistance. It was an irritant to the occupying powers because it collected and published details of German actions in France. Not the least of its influence had rested in its editorials. Now the young and popular author 'of the Absurd' was revealed to be the writer of those editorials. Camus's reputation assumed a new dimension, and fame now became an embarrassment to him. The French looked to Camus to produce from the experience of the Occupation a work which would do them proud. They expected much of him, but they could not have foreseen that in 1947 he would publish such a consummate masterpiece as *La Peste*.

4

La Peste

Of the possible responses to a discovery of the part played by
the Absurd in human endeavour, enumerated by Camus in
Le Mythe de Sisyphe, some have already found fictional illustration. Martha in *Le Malentendu* capitulated to the Absurd
by committing suicide, Caligula in the play of that name allied
himself with the Absurd against mankind by intensifying its
power. In *La Peste* the only response worthy of man, the position of revolt, is given eloquent expression. It shows how it is
possible to acknowledge the fact of the Absurd, without evasion or illusion, and yet not surrender to it. *La Peste* also
embodies an altruism absent from earlier works and barely
suggested by Cherea in *Caligula*. While *L'Etranger* showed
the individual moment of awareness, and *Le Mythe de Sisyphe*
an individual opposition against the Absurd, *La Peste* is a
portrait of collective struggle. 'Pour le moment il y a des
malades et il faut les guérir', says Rieux (p. 144). Camus has
emerged from his introspective phase, a fact which he recognized himself in a letter to Roland Barthes:

> Comparée à *L'Etranger*, *La Peste* marque sans discussion
> possible le passage d'une attitude de révolte solitaire à
> la reconnaissance d'une communauté dont il faut partager
> les luttes.[1]

La Peste is one of those rare books which are so rich that

[1] *Pléiade*, p. 1966. 'Compared to *L'Etranger*, *La Peste* does represent,
beyond any possible discussion, the movement from an attitude of
solitary revolt to the recognition of a community whose struggles must be
shared.'

they can withstand interpretation on a dozen different levels without suffering diminishment. It is a thoroughly gripping novel, an allegory with many tentacles, and a personal statement of belief. The plague itself can represent whatever the reader finds most objectionable or unendurable in human life, and is thus subject to an infinite variety of symbolic interpretations. However, one symbol can contain them all, I think, and that is the plague as a personification of the Absurd, remembering that the Absurd is Camus's shorthand word to describe the lack of reason in the human condition. This will do to start with, at least, though the image will become denser as we proceed.

There is virtually no plot. Camus describes the reactions of half a dozen characters to the advent of a plague, inviting the reader (even guiding him) to draw certain conclusions from these reactions. The relationship of the characters with each other is not examined. Camus is less interested in what people say and do to each other than in what they say and do about their ultimate destiny. He admitted as much when he wrote, in *L'Envers et L'Endroit*, 'J'ai moins appris sur les êtres parce que ma curiosité va plus à leur destin qu'à leurs réactions . . .'[1] This gives rise to a certain impersonality in the narrative, so that the reader has the impression that he is being preached at, that Camus is getting him by the shoulders, giving him a vigorous shake, and telling him to listen.

The work is described by Camus as a 'chronique', a word which implies objectivity and detachment. It is constructed with the care, shape, and beauty of a classical symphony (Mozart was Camus's great love). There are five parts, rising in length and tension until the third part, when the plague is at its apogée, and then *diminuendo* until it finally disappears. The scene is Oran, a town in Algeria, an ordinary place like anywhere else, says Camus, 'un lieu neutre'. The narrator, Dr Rieux, stumbles over a dead rat in the first sentence of the second chapter of Part I. More dead rats appear, as Camus

[1] p. 25. 'I have learnt less about people, since I am interested more in their destiny than in their reactions.'

introduces us one by one to his characters, and mysterious illnesses suggest an epidemic. Dr Rieux is the first to recognize the truth, that they have a plague on their hands, but the authorities are slow to agree. Eventually, the truth is so obvious that no one can deny it, and Camus concentrates on the attitudes towards the truth exemplified by Rieux, Tarrou, Rambert, Paneloux, Grand and Cottard. The struggle is long and arduous, Rambert and Cottard are profoundly changed as a result, Tarrou and Paneloux both die of the plague, Cottard is killed by the police. When the plague has receded, the gates of Oran are opened again, but the reader is left with an uneasy feeling that this is not the end of the matter, that the events related might occur again, somewhere else, and that they might concern him.

Camus creates this impression by insisting on the banality and ordinariness of life in Oran. 'Ce qu'il fallait souligner, c'est l'aspect banal de la ville et de la vie.'[1] The people of Oran (like the people in *L'Etranger*) are dominated by habits which have erected a screen between themselves and their awareness of life. Their existence follows a stagnant pattern, best illustrated by the little old man who amuses himself by spitting on cats from his window and who does not know what to do with himself when the plague robs him of cats (p. 130), and by the asthmatic whose day is ruled by the counting of peas. He has two saucepans; he transfers peas, one by one, from one saucepan to the other. When the exercise has been completed, he knows it is time he had something to eat (p. 133). Camus has got to create an atmosphere of boredom both to remind us that there is nothing special about Oran, and what happened there could be relevant to us, and to prepare the way for the moment of awareness when the 'décors s'écroulent' and the inhabitants are forcibly confronted with their own mortality. After a while, even the plague becomes a habit for some, such is the perversity of man's desire for security. You can get used to anything, Camus's mother used to tell him. The inhabitants

[1] p. 15. 'Really, all that was to be conveyed was the banality of the town's appearance and of life in it.'

of Oran grow accustomed to the plague, thus enabling them-selves to avoid the uncomfortable and distressing conse-quences of thinking about it. Rather than have their lives disrupted by pestilence, they will adapt to it. 'Ils s'enfermaient dans la peste.' 'Au matin, ils revenaient au fléau, c'est-à-dire à la routine.'[1]

The impression of a common experience, which the reader shares with the narrator and with the inhabitants of Oran, is further strengthened by a scrupulously objective style. In a parenthesis, Rieux confides to the reader that he has deliber-ately sought to be objective, because he did not want to distort the truth as he saw it:

> . . . pour ne rien trahir et surtout pour ne pas se trahir lui-même, le narrateur a tendu à l'objectivité. Il n'a presque rien voulu modifier par les effets de l'art.[2]

The narrator has determined to tell the truth, the whole truth, and nothing but the truth. Zola wrote that the novelist should do no more than note the facts, and this is what Rieux intends in his account.[3] Hence the horrifying details are related dis-passionately for the most part, and the reader is encouraged to feel that the events described, though ultimate in their horror, are in a way quite ordinary. 'Sur les trottoirs, il arrivait aussi à plus d'un promeneur nocturne de sentir sous son pied la masse élastique d'un cadavre encore frais.'[4] Moreover, the doctor's style is in direct relation to the clear-sighted lucidity

[1] p. 202. 'In the morning, they harked back to normal conditions, in other words, the plague.'

[2] p. 198. 'So as not to play false to the facts, and, still more, so as not to play false to himself, the narrator has aimed at objectivity. He has made hardly any changes for the sake of artistic effect.'

[3] Emile Zola, *Le Roman Expérimental* (1880): 'le romancier n'est plus qu'un greffier, qui se défend de juger et de conclure . . . l'unique besogne de l'auteur a été de mettre sous vos yeux les documents vrais.' (the novelist is no more than a clerk, who refrains from drawing conclusions or passing judgement . . . the sole duty of the author has been to submit to your examination truthful documents. BM)

[4] p. 26. 'People out at night would often feel underfoot the squelchy roundness of a still warm body.'

which Camus claims is necessary if one is to overcome the Absurd. Rieux uses language for clarification, not obfuscation as he implies some of his more conservative colleagues do. Language and style for him serve to sweep the decks clear of confusing evasions and face the truth as it is. 'C'est que les rats meurent dans la rue et les hommes dans leur chambre.'[1] In describing the death of a rat in lurid detail, Camus is setting an example; it is for the reader to apply this ruthless objectivity in his contemplation of the human predicament:

> La bête s'arrêta, sembla chercher un équilibre, prit sa course vers le docteur, s'arrêta encore, tourna sur elle-même avec un petit cri et tomba enfin en rejetant du sang par les babines entrouvertes.[2]

The Characters

1. *Dr Rieux*

Dr Rieux is by no means an extraordinary man. He has a wife and mother whom he loves, he took up medicine because it was a challenge for a working-class boy, he forgets to turn off the indicators of his car after he has turned a corner. He is modest and unassuming. Rieux is meant to represent the average man who, by nature of his work, is constantly made aware of the human predicament. Potentially, we are all Dr Rieux. *Le Mythe de Sisyphe* prepared us for him, for he is the fulfilment of the hypothetical *homme absurde* described in that essay. Rieux is the modern Sisyphus.

He thinks in terms of the present. The plague has robbed the Oranais of their future, which has suddenly been placed in doubt, but they are suffering in the present. Rieux is concerned to alleviate their present pain, in which regard he contrasts with Father Paneloux, who cares for their future salvation.

[1] p. 47. 'For rats die in the street; men in their homes.'
[2] p. 18. 'The animal stopped and seemed to be trying to get its balance, moved forward again towards the doctor, halted again, then spun round on itself with a little squeal and fell on its side. Its mouth was slightly open and blood was spurting from it.'

Paneloux s'assit près de Rieux. Il avait l'air ému.
– Oui, dit-il, oui, vous aussi vous travaillez pour le salut de l'homme.
Rieux essayait de sourire.
– Le salut de l'homme est un trop grand mot pour moi. Je ne vais pas si loin. C'est sa santé qui m'intéresse, sa santé d'abord.[1]

To care for the body and not the soul, Rieux has to concentrate on the immediate problem of dying and suffering people. He has no time to speculate why he devotes his life to caring for people; he is not a philosopher, he merely does his job:

– Ah! dit Rieux, on ne peut pas en même temps guérir et savoir. Alors guérissons le plus vite possible. C'est le plus pressé.[2]

Doing his job involves more than taking pulses. Rieux is impelled by a quiet but fierce love for his fellows and a deeply-felt anger with the suffering they are made to endure:

. . . ayant pourtant le goût de ses semblables et décidé à refuser, pour sa part, l'injustice et les concessions . . . ce qui lui tordait le cœur à ce moment était l'immense colère qui vient à l'homme devant la douleur que tous les hommes partagent.[3]

Rieux's love shows itself in unobtrusive, unremarkable ways. He visits Grand long before Grand falls ill, because he knows the man is lonely and would welcome company. He does not reproach the journalist Rambert for trying to leave Oran,

[1] p. 238. 'Paneloux sat down beside Rieux. It was obvious that he was deeply moved. "Yes, yes", he said, "you, too, are working for man's salvation." Rieux tried to smile. "Salvation's much too big a word for me. I don't aim so high. I'm concerned with man's health; and for me his health comes first." '

[2] p. 228. ' "Ah," Rieux said, "a man can't cure and *know* at the same time. So let's cure as quickly as we can. That's the more urgent job." '

[3] p. 23. 'though he had much liking for his fellow-men – and had resolved, for his part, to have no truck with injustice and compromises with the truth.'
p. 282. 'and what filled his breast was the passionate indignation we feel when confronted by the anguish all men share.'

and join the woman he loves, because, he says, 'J'ai envie, moi aussi, de faire quelque chose pour le bonheur.'[1] When Father Paneloux is dying, notwithstanding Rieux's profound distaste for the priest's views, he offers to sit by him until the end. He loves the man, but not the idea he represents. Rieux's capacity to love engenders an obstinate optimism as far as people are concerned, a conviction that 'les hommes sont plutôt bons que mauvais'.[2] Armed with this love, Rieux is strong enough to take upon his own shoulders some of the suffering he sees around him, to express a fraternal solidarity with the victims of the plague:

> ... il a pris délibérément le parti de la victime et a voulu rejoindre les hommes, ses concitoyens, dans les seules certitudes qu'ils aient en commun, et qui sont l'amour, la souffrance et l'exil. C'est ainsi qu'il n'est pas une des angoisses de ses concitoyens qu'il n'ait partagée, aucune situation qui n'ait été aussi la sienne.[3]

His love teaches him tolerance, as in his dealings with Rambert, whom he might be tempted to accuse of selfishness, but whose motives and desires he understands; he will not say that Rambert's desire for personal happiness is necessarily wrong. The only time his patience wears thin is when the priest voices the opinion that God's ways are mysterious, and we should perhaps love them without understanding them:

> Rieux se redressa d'un seul coup. Il regardait Paneloux, avec toute la force et la passion dont il était capable, et secouait la tête.
> – Non, mon père, dit-il. Je me fais une autre idée de l'amour. Et je refuserai jusqu'à la mort d'aimer cette création où les enfants sont torturés.[4]

[1] p. 222. 'I too would like to do my bit for happiness.'
[2] p. 148. 'On the whole, men are more good than bad.'
[3] p. 324. 'He has deliberately taken the victims' side and tried to share with his fellow-citizens the only certitudes they had in common – love, exile and suffering. Thus he can truly say there was not one of their anxieties in which he did not share, no predicament of theirs that was not his.'
[4] p. 238. 'Rieux straightened up slowly (Rieux sprung to attention –

But his anger is with the doctrine, not with the man. 'Les chrétiens parlent quelquefois ainsi', he says, 'sans le penser jamais réellement. Ils sont meilleurs qu'ils ne paraissent.'[1]

Rieux himself has no religious beliefs. For him, the religious attitude involves resignation, despair, and surrender, all of which are repugnant and incomprehensible to him:

> Cependant, quand on voit la misère et la douleur qu'elle apporte, il faut être fou, aveugle ou lâche pour se résigner à la peste.[2]

Besides, Rieux has no time for religion. The struggle against the plague, and by implication the struggle with life, occupy all his efforts. 'Il fallait lutter de telle ou telle façon et ne pas se mettre à genoux.'[3] Rieux's concern is with people and their lives, not with ideas and abstractions. If Paneloux had seen more suffering, he says, he would not talk so glibly of The Light. Rieux's whole effort is to speak with clarity and emphasis and to resist the cunning mantle of deceit thrown up by the misuse of language. When trying to persuade the authorities to declare an emergency he encounters their stubborn reluctance to call a spade a spade. It does not matter whether you call it a plague or not, he says, as long as you prevent it from killing half the town (p. 62). Rieux will have no compromise with abstract concepts which conceal the facts. He insists on vigilance and honesty at all times:

> Ce qu'il fallait faire, c'était reconnaître clairement ce qui

---

BM). He gazed at Paneloux, summoning to his gaze all the strength and fervour he could muster against his weariness. Then he shook his head. "No, Father. I've a very different ideal of love. And until my dying day I shall refuse to love a scheme of things in which children are put to torture."'

[1] p. 142. 'Christians sometimes say that sort of thing without really thinking it. They're better than they seem.'

[2] p. 142. 'All the same, when you see the misery it brings, you'd need to be a madman, or a coward, or stone blind, to give in tamely to the plague.'

[3] p. 150. 'Their certitude that a fight must be put up, in this way or that, and there must be no bowing down.'

devait être reconnu, chasser enfin les ombres inutiles et prendre les mesures qui convenaient.[1]

There is a long conversation with Rambert in which Rieux explains his conception of honesty, a kind of integrity before the facts such as we perceive in *L'Etranger* and *Le Mythe de Sisyphe*:

> il ne s'agit pas d'héroisme dans tout cela. Il s'agit d'honnêteté. C'est une idée qui peut faire rire, mais la seule façon de lutter contre la peste, c'est l'honnêteté.
> – Qu'est-ce que l'honnêteté, dit Rambert, d'un air soudain sérieux.
> – Je ne sais pas ce qu'elle est en général.
> Mais dans mon cas, je sais qu'elle consiste à faire mon métier.[2]

Why such an insistence on facing the facts? Because you cannot deal with them until you recognize them and because concealment of the facts generally gives rise to evil committed in ignorance and error (p. 148). Rieux does not regard his hard struggle against the plague as in any way heroic. For him it is a natural consequence of the situation in which he finds himself. The plague is there, *ergo* it must be fought. There is nothing admirable in this; it is a matter of course that men will side with men against a calamity which threatens them all. To Tarrou, who talks of sanctity, Rieux has this to say:

> je me sens plus de solidarité avec les vaincus qu'avec les saints. Je n'ai pas de goût, je crois, pour l'héroisme et la sainteté. Ce qui m'intéresse, c'est d'être un homme.[3]

[1] p. 53. 'It was only a matter of lucidly recognizing what had to be recognized; of dispelling extraneous shadows and doing what needed to be done.'

[2] p. 180. ' "There's no question of heroism in all this. It's a matter of common decency. That's an idea which may make some people smile, but the only means of fighting a plague is – common decency." "What do you mean by common decency?" Rambert's tone was grave. "I don't know what it means for other people, but in my case I know it consists in doing my job." '

[3] p. 276. 'I feel more fellowship with the defeated than with saints. Heroism and sanctity don't really appeal to me, I imagine. What interests me is – being a man.'

Although Rieux denies that he is heroic, there is definitely a certain stoicism in his persistent efforts against incredible odds. He has no illusions about the efficacy of his work. He knows that all the victims of the plague will die, in spite of his medicine. His wife dies in a sanatorium in another town without his being able to see her again. His friend Tarrou dies. Devoid of illusion, he trudges from one death-bed to another. Day after day the smell of death, the sound of death, the desperate hysterical pleas of wives and mothers who cling to his arm and beg him to work some magic, every day in vain, and every day repeated. Like Sisyphus labouring with his rock up the self-perpetuating hill, Rieux has the bitter knowledge that his task is doomed to failure:

> Et au bout de cette longue suite de soirs toujours semblables, Rieux ne pouvait espérer rien d'autre qu'une longue suite de scènes pareilles, indéfiniment renouvelées.[1]

Like Sisyphus, he will not give up simply because he knows he cannot succeed. Each victim is a new rock to be pushed to the summit. There is no romanticism in this hero:

> Mais vos victoires seront provisoires, voilà tout. Rieux parut s'assombrir.
> – Toujours, je le sais. Ce n'est pas une raison pour cesser de lutter.
> – Non, ce n'est pas une raison. Mais j'imagine alors ce que doit être cette peste pour vous.
> – Oui, dit Rieux. Une interminable défaite.[2]

Rieux goes on because he is in rebellion against the injustice of the plague; to do otherwise would be to succomb to it. He represents the position of revolt which is lucid yet indomitable. At the same time, because Camus wants Rieux to be a man like other men, and not a cypher, one must not forget that

[1] p. 105. 'Rieux had nothing to look forward to but a long sequence of such scenes, renewed again and again.'
[2] p. 145. ' "But your victories will never be lasting; that's all." Rieux's face darkened. "Yes, I know that. But it's no reason for giving up the struggle." "No reason, I agree. . . . Only, I now can picture what this plague must mean for you." "Yes. A never-ending defeat." '

he is a creature of emotion. He allows that he feels a need for human warmth (p. 70), and he tells Rambert that nothing warrants neglecting one's love. One day, the relative of a victim accused him of being heartless. No, he said, he did have a heart. His heart gave him the strength to withstand the spectacle, twenty hours a day, of men who should be alive dying before his eyes (p. 210). Rieux is an anti-hero, if you like. But his quiet, steadfast love of life in the midst of evil and destruction shines like a lighted window seen through the midnight fog.

2. *Tarrou*

Tarrou is a visitor to Oran, nobody knows quite from where. Caught in the plague, he takes upon himself the organization of emergency services and is soon Rieux's staunchest ally in his struggle. He bears many similarities to Rieux and to the ideal *homme absurde*. He enjoys a life of the senses, was frequently to be found on the beach, before the plague, swimming with manifest pleasure. Like Rieux, he prefers to love men than to define them (p. 277). He accepts without question his commitment to the struggle and is totally selfless in his devotion to what he sees as a common duty to defend men against an obscene threat to their dignity. Like Rieux, he values his lucidity and works constantly to combat the mystifications of language. He believes that 'tout le malheur des hommes venait de ce qu'ils ne tenaient pas un langage clair. J'ai pris le parti alors de parler et d'agir clairement.'[1] A real friendship soon grows between the two men who at one point take time off from the struggle, during which Tarrou explains his past. What Tarrou then relates is the history of a specific 'moment of awareness'. He had been the son of a public prosecutor and was himself intended for a career at the bar. When he was seventeen, he sat through a murder trial in which his father took part. He was overcome with horror at the spectacle of the cowering, frightened defendant, now alive,

[1] p. 275. 'All our troubles spring from our failure to use plain, clean-cut language. So I resolved always to speak, and to act, quite clearly.'

who would soon be made dead in the name of official justice. Tarrou could not bring himself to think in terms of judicial retribution, a semantic device which would allow him to watch the disgusting procedure with a clear conscience. He could only think that the man's neck was to be broken. 'J'ai cru que la société où je vivais était celle qui reposait sur la condamnation à mort et qu'en la combattant, je combattrais l'assassinat.'[1] In his anguish, he joined a group of political dissidents but was horrified to find that they too, in fighting for the dignity and honour of man, killed men who did not agree with them. He describes to Rieux what it is like to see a man executed by a firing squad. The rifle is only four feet away from the wretched man's chest, and when the shot is fired, there is a hole in him into which you can place your fist. Sadly, Tarrou concluded that absolute justice was impossible, and that he would play no part in political action which intensified the misfortunes of men. Retaining his moral idealism, yet knowing that it was unrealizable, Tarrou's troubled conscience was made to settle for compromise; he would strive to remain relatively un-contaminated, to do as little harm as possible to men, and perhaps occasionally, with luck, to do a little good (p. 273). He would try to be an 'innocent murderer':

> Si, disant cela, je deviens fléau moi-même, du moins, je n'y suis pas consentant. J'essaie d'être un meurtrier innocent. Vous voyez que ce n'est pas une grande am-bition. . . . C'est pourquoi j'ai décidé de me mettre du côté des victimes, en toute occasion, pour limiter les dégâts.[2]

Tarrou is a sensitive man with an acutely tortured conscience which will not give him peace. To the plague brought by the

[1] p. 271. 'To my mind the social order around me was based on the death-sentence, and by fighting the established order I'd be fighting against murder.'

[2] p. 275. 'If, by making that statement, I, too, become a carrier of the plague-germ, at least I don't do it wilfully. I try, in short, to be an innocent murderer. You see, I've no great ambitions. . . . That's why I decided to take, in every predicament, the victim's side – so as to reduce the damage done.'

rats corresponds, in his view, an inner plague with which we are all tainted, and which manifests itself in hatred, intolerance, and deceit. The fight against these evils must be life-long; 'chacun la porte en soi, la peste, parce que personne, non, personne au monde n'en est indemne'.[1] While wishing with all his soul to be an optimist, Tarrou finds it difficult to avoid pessimism. Men will reveal goodness if given the opportunity, he says; the trouble is, they so often die before they have the chance. The most that he can do is to side, wherever possible, against the evil inherent in human life. His is another position of revolt:

> Je dis seulement qu'il y a sur cette terre des fléaux et des victimes et qu'il faut, autant qu'il est possible, refuser d'être avec le fléau.[2]

Where Tarrou differs from Rieux is in his obstinate idealism. Rieux has no illusions; Tarrou continues to cherish one, that he might purge himself from the inevitable taint of evil. He would like to believe that purity is possible:

> – En somme, dit Tarrou avec simplicité, ce qui m'intéresse, c'est de savoir comment on devient un saint.
> – Mais vous ne croyez pas en Dieu.
> – Justement. Peut-on être un saint sans Dieu, c'est le seul problème concret que je connaisse aujourd'hui.[3]

In other words, how is one to prevent the hopelessness of the human predicament from gnawing into one's soul? Can one prevent the lucidity of the intelligent 'aware' man from developing into a cancer? Tarrou aims too high. He is finally brought to realize the limitations of the position of revolt and

[1] p. 274. 'each of us has the plague within him; no one, on earth, is free from it.'

[2] p. 274. 'All I maintain is that on this earth there are pestilences and there are victims, and it's up to us, so far as possible, not to join forces with the pestilences.'

[3] p. 276. ' "It comes to this," Tarrou said almost casually, "what interests me is learning how to become a saint." "But you don't believe in God." "Exactly! Can one be a saint without God? – that's the problem, in fact the only problem, I'm up against today." '

to acknowledge that, while he cannot aspire to do good, he must retain his lucidity and do as little harm as possible. His attitude is finely defined in Camus's later essay, *L'Homme Révolté*:

> La logique du révolté est de vouloir servir la justice pour ne pas ajouter à l'injustice de la condition, de s'efforcer au langage clair pour ne pas épaissir le mensonge universel et de parier, face à la douleur des hommes, pour le bonheur.[1]

3. *Rambert*

Rambert is the one character with whom the reader can most readily sympathize. He is a journalist from Paris on an assignment when the plague erupts and he finds himself trapped in Oran. He protests that he is a 'special case', that he does not belong to Oran, and that the town's problem is none of his business. He wants to go home to Paris, and to the woman with whom he is very much in love. The plague, however, does not discriminate. It is worthwhile noting that Camus was himself forcibly separated from his wife by the circumstances of the war; when he was in France, from 1942, she was exiled in distant Oran. This alone is sufficient indication that Camus understands the predicament of Rambert, and paints his portrait with sympathy. Rambert is a part of Camus, just as Tarrou and Rieux are parts of Camus.

Rambert is a robust man, 'sportif', sensual. A veteran of the Spanish Civil War, in which he fought on the side of the vanquished Republicans, he has long since abandoned any illusion that ideologies, of whatever colour, can provide a solution to human anguish. He now sees ideological zeal as destructive; he has resolved never again to fight for an idea. The Plague is an idea, 'an abstraction'. He resists what he sees as the dehumanizing effect that the pestilence has on Rieux (though he is wrong in his assessment). For Rambert, only one thing matters in life, and that is affection, or feeling, or 'being

[1] p. 342. 'The logic of the rebel is to want to serve justice so as not to add to the injustice of the human condition, to insist on plain language so as not to increase the universal falsehood and to wager, in spite of human misery, for happiness.'

in love'. The experience of sharing one's life with another person, to the extent that you take on the skin of that person, feel the same joys, tremble at the same fears, share the same apprehensions, this is what life is about. If a man has not had a great love, then his life has been wasted:

> Maintenant je sais que l'homme est capable de grandes actions. Mais s'il n'est capable d'un grand sentiment, il ne m'intéresse pas.[1]

Rambert speaks for all those who are happy in love, who have found a reason for living in the generosity of human emotion, in union with another creature. The plague threatens to destroy his reason for living, to make a mockery of his life. If he must die, he wants to die for love, not for an impersonal, abstract, incomprehensible pestilence, which is none of his concern in the first place:

> Eh bien moi, j'en ai assez des gens qui meurent pour une idée. Je ne crois pas à l'héroisme, je sais que c'est facile et j'ai appris que c'était meurtrier. Ce qui m'intéresse, c'est qu'on vive et qu'on meure de ce qu'on aime.[2]

Rambert's is a stand for personal happiness. Rieux does not blame him for this. As we have seen, Rieux is fully in agreement that nothing in the world justifies neglecting one's love. He does not try to prevent Rambert from escaping. He wishes him luck. But he does point out that man is not an idea, and from that moment Rambert is troubled. He asks if Rieux would accept his help in the emergency services until such time as he finds a way of escape. When the opportunity to escape does finally present itself, Rambert elects to stay with Rieux and Tarrou. *La Peste*, I have said, was the first of Camus's books to recognize the part of altruism in human affairs, and that part is illustrated specifically by Rambert, who sacrifices what he most believes in for the intangible imperative of human solidarity. Rieux remonstrates with him, insisting that it is stupid to be ashamed

---

[1] p. 179. 'I know now that man is capable of great deeds. But if he isn't capable of a great emotion, well, he leaves me cold.'

[2] p. 179. 'Well, personally, I've seen enough of people who die for an idea. I don't believe in heroism; I know it's easy and I've learnt it can be murderous. What interests me is living and dying for what one loves.'

of wanting personal happiness. 'Oui, dit Rambert, mais il peut y avoir de la honte à être heureux tout seul'.[1] In terms of the values postulated in *Le Mythe de Sisyphe*, Rambert has discovered that the position of revolt against the human condition, personified by the plague, is not a choice but an inevitability:

> Mais maintenant que j'ai vu ce que j'ai vu, je sais que je suis d'ici, que je le veuille ou non. Cette histoire nous concerne tous.[2]

4. *Grand*

Joseph Grand is allowed a more detailed description than any other character (pp. 56–9, 282–4). Paradoxically, he is the most insignificant. A modest pen-pushing civil servant, clumsy in speech and in personal relationships, unable to express himself properly, Grand has 'toutes les mines de l'insignifiance'. His life has been trivialized by sterile routine, every day, week and year mournfully predictable. His story was perfectly simple, he said, 'il en est ainsi pour tout le monde: on se marie, on aime encore un peu, on travaille. On travaille tant qu'on en oublie d'aimer.'[3] Like many a nonentity, Grand longs to make the world sit up and take notice of him. He will write the perfect book. For years he has been working on this book, but has progressed no further than the first sentence, which he subjects to endless revisions in his quest after perfection. We should be wary of looking with scorn upon Grand's literary endeavour, however, because I suspect Camus intends it to be exemplary. Fruitless though his efforts be, Grand's clumsy attempt at artistic creation casts him in the mould of one of the four types of *homme absurde* enumerated in *Le Mythe de Sisyphe* (see above, p. 53). He arouses sympathy because his life has suffered from his being inarticulate. He is the kind of

[1] p. 227. 'Certainly, Rambert replied. But it may be shameful to be happy by oneself.'

[2] p. 228. 'But now that I've seen what I have seen, I know that I belong here whether I want it or not. This business is everybody's business.'

[3] p. 97. 'The common lot of married couples. You get married, you go on loving a bit longer, you work. And you work so hard that it makes you forget to love.'

inoffensive little man, not gifted with eloquence and therefore likely to pass unnoticed, for whom Camus felt profound regard, and to whom he pays tribute in this character. Had Grand been able to 'find the right word' he would have been a happily married man. His wife Jeanne, whom he married very young, deserted him because she was unable to perceive that he loved her in spite of his crippling inability to put his love into words. 'Tant que nous nous sommes aimés, nous nous sommes compris sans paroles. Mais on ne s'aime pas toujours. A un moment donné, j'aurais dû trouver les mots qui l'auraient retenue, mais je n'ai pas pu.'[1] When Grand talks to Rieux about his wife, he weeps with the burden of loneliness. He feels the same need for human tenderness as Rambert. Moreover, he does not disguise his emotion. Grand is admirable by his very normality; he is honest and devoid of pretentiousness or deceit:

> Il était de ces hommes, rares dans notre ville comme ailleurs, qui ont toujours le courage de leurs bons sentiments. Le peu qu'il confiait de lui témoignait en effet de bontés et d'attachements qu'on n'ose pas avouer de nos jours.[2]

Grand's part in the common struggle is to keep a statistical record of the sanitary operations. This is the job for which his modest talents are most suited and he tackles the work without question and with quiet, resolute courage. His is the simplest form of revolt and in many ways the best. It does not occur to him that one could *not* revolt. Not for Grand the soul-searching of Tarrou or the conflict of interests which torment Rambert: 'il y a la peste,' he says, 'il faut se défendre, c'est clair. Ah! si tout était aussi simple!'[3] The narrator, Rieux, makes no secret

---

p. 98. 'While we loved each other we didn't need words to make ourselves understood. But people don't love forever. A time came when I should have found the words to keep her with me – only I couldn't.'

[2] p. 58. 'He was one of those rare people, rare in our town as elsewhere, who have the courage of their good feelings. What little he told of his personal life vouched for acts of kindness and a capacity for affection which no one in our times dares to own to.'

[3] p. 151. 'Plague is here and we've got to make a stand, that's obvious. Ah, I only wish everything were as simple.'

of his admiration for this humble man and considers that if there must be a hero in his story, it is this 'héros insignifiant et effacé' who accepts his commitment without fuss. He comes nearest to Tarrou's almost impossible ideal of 'sanctity without God'.

Joseph Grand catches the plague, but survives. The experience of human solidarity and communal effort has left upon him a mark which will not easily be erased. He burns his abortive manuscript and starts a letter to his estranged wife. The memory of her is now a source of pleasure to him. One is left with the impression that his life has been enriched and that he will start afresh.

5. *Cottard*

Cottard is another lonely figure, a wine salesman by trade, withdrawn, solitary and distrustful. He has committed an unspecified crime for which he is wanted by the police and consequently lives in fear and apprehension, talking to no one, shut up with his guilt. 'C'est un homme,' says Grand, 'qui a quelque chose à se reprocher.'[1] Grand elsewhere calls him 'le désespéré', which gives us a clue to his significance in the story. In *Le Mythe de Sisyphe* Camus listed unacceptable responses to an awareness of the misery of human life – suicide, despair, acquiescence and resignation (or metaphysical hope). Of these, Cottard is guilty of the first three, and Paneloux of the last. We do not know exactly what the man has done, but it is intimated that his crime was the result, not the cause, of his despair. He was unpopular, unable to achieve contact with other people, misunderstood and neglected. At the beginning of the book, he attempts to kill himself. The only reason this reticent man will give is 'personal problems' (*chagrins intimes*). He has abdicated to despair in his empty life.

The advent of the plague effects a profound transformation in his behaviour. He glories in it, turns it to his own advantage by selfish exploitation of the situation, grows rich on sordid, petty black-market dealings. 'Je m'y trouve bien, moi, dans

[1] p. 70. 'He's a man who has something to reproach himself for.'

la peste,' he tells Tarrou, 'et je ne vois pas pourquoi je me mêlerais de la faire cesser.'[1] Hence his second, far worse, crime, which is complacent acquiescence in the disaster. He is on the side of the plague, against its victims: 'Car visiblement c'est un complice et un complice qui se délecte.'[2]

Camus presents the portrait of Cottard in such a way that we are led not to despise him but to pity him. The reasons for his alliance with the forces of evil are simple and pathetic. He was lonely before, under an individual threat which isolated him. Now the threat is general, 'tout le monde est dans le bain'[3] and he can feel the comfort of walking shoulder to shoulder with his fellows. More than anything, he wants human warmth, he wants people to like him, and the plague, a common enemy which erases all previous distinctions, places him on the same level with everyone else. He becomes garrulous and gregarious, mixes with the crowd, initiates conversations. His morbid self-absorption disappears. No wonder he welcomes the plague; it gives him a new lease of life:

> La seule chose qu'il ne veuille pas, c'est d'être séparé des autres. Il préfère être assiégé avec tous que prisonnier tout seul.[4]

Tarrou, from whose notebooks we learn these details of Cottard's behaviour, does not think there is any real malice in his character (p. 216). He blames him for having refused rebellion and sided with the plague, but is ready to forgive him: 'Son seul vrai crime, c'est d'avoir approuvé dans son cœur ce qui faisait mourir des enfants et des hommes.'[5] There is no greater measure of Camus's love and tolerance than this

[1] p. 175. 'What's more, the plague suits me quite well and I see no reason why I should bother about trying to stop it.'

[2] p. 215. 'Yes, "accomplice" is the word that fits, and doesn't he relish his complicity!'

[3] p. 213. 'everyone's in the same boat'.

[4] p. 213. 'The thing he'd most detest is being cut off from others; he'd rather be one of a beleaguered crowd than a prisoner alone.'

[5] p. 325. 'His only real crime is that of having in his heart approved of something that killed off men, women and children.'

portrait of a man whose actions he cannot condone but is ready to ascribe to fear and ignorance rather than malevolence.

With the waning of the epidemic, Cottard becomes more and more desperate, reverts to his former neurosis, and finally barricades himself in his flat, from which he shoots wildly at the crowd. He kills a dog, and is in turn killed by the police.

6. *Paneloux*

Father Paneloux is a Jesuit priest, educated and intelligent, a likeable man widely respected in Oran, even by non-Christians. He delivers two sermons during the course of the plague, separated by an experience which provokes a crisis of conscience.

The first sermon, delivered with the vigour of profound conviction, presents the plague as an instance of divine retribution. 'Mes frères, vous êtes dans le malheur, mes frères, vous l'avez mérité',[1] he says. This is the traditionally militant Christian position based on the concept of Original Sin, according to which we are all inherently guilty and natural catastrophes have a punitive purpose. As Egypt was punished, so now it is the turn of Oran to feel the wrath of God. Hence for Paneloux there is no mystery about the epidemic, it conforms to the order arranged by God. Suffering is thereby rationalized and given a meaning; it is no longer an inexplicable outrage. It follows, in Paneloux's sermon, that we can benefit from the disaster, look into ourselves to find where our fault lies, and learn to deserve God's mercy. It is an opportunity to be uplifted: 'Ce fléau même qui vous meurtrit, il vous élève et vous montre la voie.'[2] Paneloux's message is that the proper response to the pestilence is not to revolt but to submit to God's will; He, in His wisdom, will put an end to the suffering when the time is ripe. We must hope against hope and place our trust in God.

[1] p. 110. 'Calamity has come on you, my brethren, and, my brethren, you have deserved it.'

[2] p. 113. 'This same pestilence which is slaying you works for your good and points your path.'

Rieux's view, as we have seen, is that Paneloux can think only in abstractions. Fidelity to the logic of his ideas prevents him from seeing the reality that those ideas conceal. He is the victim of his own obfuscated language. Where Tarrou and Rieux strive to speak with clarity about life as it is, Paneloux speaks with rhetoric about an idea of life. Where Paneloux talks of God, and Man, and Punishment, Rieux and Tarrou see only people dying in agony. If he had spent as much time in hospitals as I have, comments Rieux laconically, he would not be so ready to talk of retribution. Paneloux agrees to join forces with Rieux and his associates, but he is motivated not by love of men, but by an idea of Christian Duty. The implication is that Paneloux would be far more useful if he could bring himself to refrain from sermons which excite fear and prey on guilt and so divert the efforts of his followers from the job in hand, which is to beat the plague. Paneloux, though sincere, is a harmful and divisive influence.

There then comes the painful and poignant scene in which the death agony of Judge Othon's child is described. Both Rieux and Paneloux are present. Paneloux is visibly shaken. He kneels by the bedside and prays: 'My God, save this child.' The sweating, screaming child eventually falls silent and dies. The doctor and the priest are for once drawn together in grief. It is then that Rieux cries out, 'Ah! that one at least was innocent, you well know', and Paneloux protests that he too was revolted by the spectacle. At the end of the passage, Rieux takes the priest's hand in a moving gesture of unity. We are allies whether you like it or not, he says, not even God can separate us now.

Paneloux's second sermon is marked with mellowness and humility. He is a chastened man. No longer does he thump the pulpit and pour out a torrent of self-confident rhetoric. Instead of addressing the congregation as 'you', he talks of 'we'. His message now is one of abject resignation. Now that he has beheld the ravages of evil, he can no longer talk about it so glibly. He confesses that he does not understand but recommends that we must accept the scandalous spectacle of human suffering and trust in the mysterious ways of God. Paneloux's second sermon is a reiteration of his comment to Rieux over the body of Othon's boy: 'Mais peut-être devons-nous aimer ce que nous ne pouvons pas comprendre.'[1] To do otherwise would be to place in question his entire faith, and Paneloux recoils from this ultimatum. 'Il faut tout croire ou tout nier. Et qui donc, parmi vous, oserait tout nier?'[2] The priest must retain his idea of a good and just God at all costs, even if it means allowing the evidence of human suffering. Paneloux has lost his certainty but clings on to his faith. He has no alternative, says Tarrou:

> Quand l'innocence a les yeux crevés, un chrétien doit perdre la foi ou accepter d'avoir les yeux crevés. Paneloux ne veut pas perdre la foi, il ira jusqu'au bout.[3]

The logic of Paneloux's position demands that he take the only path left open to him, that of self-imposed humiliation, born of love of God. He must abandon himself to the divine will, though it be incomprehensible, even overtly cruel. 'L'amour de Dieu est un amour difficile. Il suppose l'abandon totale de soi-mème et le dédain de sa personne.'[4]

The good and distressed priest falls ill. True to his own teaching, he bravely refuses medical aid: the plague being sent by God, he must succumb to it. He offers no resistance. He dies clutching his crucifix. It is not certain that his death is caused by the plague. The symptoms are unusual. Is it possible that he willed his own death?

*　　　*　　　*

[1] p. 238. 'But perhaps we should love what we cannot understand.'

[2] p. 244. 'We must believe everything or deny everything. And who, I ask, amongst you would dare to deny everything?'

[3] p. 249. 'When innocence has its face smashed, a good Christian must either lose his faith or accept smashed faces. Paneloux doesn't want to lose his faith, he'll go to the bitter end.' (BM)

[4] p. 248. 'The love of God is a hard love. It demands total self-surrender, disdain of our human personality.'

Moral

The moral to be drawn from *La Peste* is evidently directly opposed to the moral of Christian doctrine, and this opposition is very neatly epitomized in the conflicting views of Rieux the doctor (pragmatic, relativist, concerned with the immediate, humanist), and Paneloux the priest (dogmatic, absolutist, concerned with the future, theist). I said earlier that one of Camus's most engaging qualities was his uncertainty: his thought was constantly alive, constantly evolving, and never afraid to absorb fresh ideas. This must now be qualified. In the matter of religion he never wavered. There is not the slightest trace of any religious feeling in his work. Camus's agnosticism was refreshingly free of dogma. 'Mes passions d'homme n'ont jamais été "contre" ',[1] he wrote in the preface to *L'Envers et L'Endroit*. He was in no way a militant or polemical atheist. A clearer definition of his position would be to describe him not as an 'anti-Christian' but as a 'non-Christian'. He would even prefer the order of premisses to be reversed, so that Christians were regarded as 'non-humanist'. He did not feel obliged to attack Christianity with violence; he regarded the idea as irrelevant, and its adherents as mistaken. In 1948 Camus was invited by the Dominicans of Latour-Maubourg to deliver an address. It his speech on that occasion, a measured and tolerant account of his position, he declared that since he did not feel possessed of absolute truth, he could not presume to state that Christian revelation was wrong:

> je ne partirai jamais du principe que la vérité chrétienne est illusoire, mais seulement de ce fait que je n'ai pu y entrer.[2]

Again, in an interview published in *Le Monde* on 31 August 1956, he reiterated the point that Christian experience was closed to him. He said he admired the life and death of Christ,

---

[1] 'My human passions have never been directed against other people.'
[2] 'I shall never start from the supposition that Christian truth is illusory, but merely from the fact that I could not accept it.'

but 'mon manque d'imagination m'interdit de le suivre plus loin'.[1] I should prefer to call it not a lack of imagination so much as a lack of fantasy. Camus's vision was resolutely earthbound. His position, therefore, was not that of an arrogant crusader, but of a man who spoke from 'outside' religious experience, while still respecting those who were 'inside' ('un esprit extérieur à la religion, mais respectueux de la conviction d'autrui'[2]). Notice how the portrait of Paneloux is drawn with charity and understanding; nowhere is it suggested that the priest is an evil man, only that he is seduced by the fallacious logic of an erroneous doctrine. Tarrou says that he is a better man than his sermons; Rieux says that Christians are sometimes given to talking in this way, but they do not really mean what they say. Camus is not here questioning the *sincerity* of Christians, but their *clarity*. He supposes that were they to listen carefully to the import of what they were saying, they could not but be appalled. The obstinacy of Christian belief he does not assign to hypocrisy but to the seduction of rhetoric, the beguiling attraction of a rounded, absolute vision which, as in a jigsaw puzzle, provides all the answers. In his address to the Dominicans, Camus regretted that no loud protest came from the Pope against the atrocities of the Second World War. He was told that the Pope had indeed issued an unequivocal condemnation. But, says Camus, he employed the language of the encyclical, which no one understands.[3] The Pope's utterance had been wrapped in the muddy eloquence of abstractions, and no one could be sure whether or not he had even noticed the bloody sufferings of the faithful. Camus reproaches the religious body for protecting itself from the truth by cloaking it in rhetoric. He does not demand any special conduct from the Christian, only that his conduct should at least be no worse than that of a non-Christian. When a Spanish bishop blesses

---

[1] 'My lack of imagination prevents me from following him any further.'
[2] *Actuelles* I, p. 46. 'A mind exterior to religion, but respectful of the convictions of others.'
[3] See also *Combat*, 26 December 1944, in the Pléiade *Essais*, p. 283.

political executions, it is not as a bishop, or a Christian, that Camus condemns him, but as a man.

When we turn from the Christian to the idea of Christianity, we find Camus rather less tolerant. He deplores the pessimism inherent in the Christian view of the world. By what right can a Christian accuse me of pessimism? he asked the Dominicans:

> Ce n'est pas moi qui ai inventé la misère de la créature, ni les terribles formules de la malédiction divine. Ce n'est pas moi qui ai crié ce *Nemo bonus*, ni la damnation des enfants sans baptême. Ce n'est pas moi qui ai dit que l'homme était incapable de se sauver tout seul et que du fond de son abaissement il n'avait d'espérance que dans la grâce de Dieu.[1]

There is in *Caligula* a trenchant satire on Christian pessimism. The Emperor has taken absolute power and made himself God. In this speech of Hélicon, if we replace Caligula on each occasion by the word God, we have a simple and direct summary of the doctrine of Divine Omnipotence:

> L'exécution soulage et délivre. Elle est universelle, fortifiante et juste dans ses applications comme dans ses intentions. On meurt parce qu'on est coupable. On est coupable parce qu'on est sujet de Caligula. Or, tout le monde est sujet de Caligula. Donc, tout le monde est coupable. D'où il ressort que tout le monde meurt. C'est une question de temps et de patience.[2]

Christianity allows for the presence of injustice in the world, which amounts to condoning it. To accept the Christian revel-

---

[1] 'I was not the one to invent the misery of the human being, or the terrifying formulas of divine malediction. I was not the one to shout *Nemo bonus* or the damnation of unbaptized children. I was not the one who said that man was incapable of saving himself by his own means and that from the depths of his degradation his only hope was in the grace of God.'

[2] Act II, Scene 9, p. 165. 'Execution relieves and liberates. It is universal, tonic, just in precept and in practice. A man dies because he is guilty. A man is guilty because he is one of Caligula's subjects. Now all men are Caligula's subjects. *Ergo*, all men are guilty and shall die. It is only a matter of time and patience.'

ation is to accept that evil, suffering, and death of innocent children are all part of the Divine Plan. 'La vérité jaillira de l'apparente injustice,' says Paneloux.[1] Even if God did exist, Camus would still refuse His creation, as long as it included injustice (*Homme Révolté*, p. 76). Moreover, the Christian view of man is a humiliating one; if he is good, it is God who takes the credit for having bestowed his grace; if he is bad, it is his own fault, or the fault of Adam. Humiliating, and also debilitating, the Christian preoccupation deflects the attention of men from their earthly existence, and thereby weakens their resolve to live well.

Camus regards any doctrine or body of belief which claims a monopoly on the truth as totalitarian. Christianity is totalitarian because its revealed truth is absolute and eternal, and demands the adherence of blind faith. As Paneloux said, you must either accept it all or reject it all; there are no half measures. Camus sees no qualitative difference between Christian and Marxist totalitarianism; they are both alike insults to the dignity and integrity of man. And, because they demand such total adherence, absolute doctrines such as Marxism and Christianity are likely to propagate evil rather than dispel it, since they encourage fanaticism and preclude debate. Camus says to the Christians, neither you nor I can alter the fact that the world is unjust, but please try not to add to the injustice!

Camus was not the first, of course, to be perplexed by the intrinsic paradox of Christian belief. If there is a God, He is either omnipotent, as the doctrine tells us, and therefore malicious (because He allows suffering and cruelty in His world), or, if He is benevolent, He is powerless (because He has not made his benevolence effective). He is either cruel or incompetent – He cannot logically be both. Faced with philosophic games such as this, Camus shows his impatience. Such discussions are sterile, he says, let us get on with the business in hand, which is to live the life we have and limit, as far as possible, the potency of evil. In the words of Rieux,

[1] p. 248. 'Truth will flash forth from the dark cloud of seeming injustice.'

> puisque l'ordre du monde est réglé par la mort, peut-être
> vaut-il mieux pour Dieu qu'on ne croie pas en lui et qu'on
> lutte de toutes ses forces contre la mort, sans lever les
> yeux vers le ciel où il se tait.[1]

Camus is happy to respect Christians from the outside while
deploring their doctrine, and to seek out and cherish what
he has in common with them rather than what divides him
from them (cf. Rieux and Paneloux). But this, on condition
that they do not allow their absolutism to foster fanatics, and
that they do not spread false hope in a future life. We have
seen often enough that Camus was irritated by the evangelist
encouragement of a useless hope, which he regarded as an
insult to life. 'S'il y a un péché contre la vie', he wrote in *Noces*,
'ce n'est peut-être pas tant d'en désespérer que d'espérer une
autre vie, et se dérober à l'implacable grandeur de celle-ci.'[2] In
Lettres à un Ami Allemand he comments that it is not much
help to a man you are about to kill [in war] to treat him to a
discourse on the afterlife (p. 42). It is extraordinary, in view of
Camus's unambiguous attitude towards the Christian revelation, that he has always had a following among Christians.
Christian commentators have thought they detected a spirit
ripe for conversion. I confess I cannot see how. I suspect it is
because they smelt the scent of pessimism, and a pessimist is
generally ripe for entry into the Church. But we cannot insist
too heavily on the point. Camus was not a pessimistic man; he
was a realist who had no time for metaphysical fantasy. He
put the point himself very finely when talking to the Dominican
friars who had invited him:

> Si le christianisme est pessimiste quant à l'homme, il est
> optimiste quant à la destinée humaine. Eh bien! je dirai

[1] p. 145. 'Since the order of the world is shaped by death, mightn't it be
better for God if we refuse to believe in Him, and struggle with all our
might against death, without raising our eyes towards the Heaven where
he sits in silence?'

[2] 'If there is a sin against life, it is perhaps not so much to despair of it,
but to hope for another life, and thus rob oneself of the implacable grandeur
of the life we have.'

que pessimiste quant à la destinée humaine, je suis optimiste quant à l'homme.[1]

* * *

Notwithstanding Camus's distaste for Christian revelation, he has a faith of his own, which, in the end, is just as irrational. It is a faith in mankind. It differs from Christian belief in that it is firmly anchored to the present and to *this* life, but otherwise it demands a 'leap of faith' almost as inexplicable. I shall avoid the word 'Humanism' as far as possible, since Camus specifically disavowed the 'narrow certainties' of the Humanists, but the fact is that his values are entirely centred on man, his worth, his potential, his misfortunes. For once, we can really talk of a *love* of man and know that we have chosen the right word. In *L'Exil et le Royaume* he talks of 'the beautiful noise that people make', and he is not merely being poetic. The *Lettres à un Ami Allemand* are a hymn to this love. Listen to this passage:

> Je continue à croire que ce monde n'a pas de sens supérieur. Mais je sais que quelque chose en lui a du sens et c'est l'homme, parce qu'il est le seul être à exiger d'en avoir. Ce monde a du moins la vérité de l'homme et notre tâche est de lui donner ses raisons contre le destin lui-même. Et il n'a pas d'autres raisons que l'homme et c'est celui-ci qu'il faut sauver si l'on veut sauver l'idée qu'on se fait de la vie. Votre sourire et votre dédain me diront: qu'est-ce sauver l'homme? Mais je vous crie de tout moi-même, c'est ne pas le mutiler et c'est donner ses chances à la justice qu'il est le seul à concevoir.[2]

[1] 'If Christianity is pessimistic as to man, it is optimistic as to human destiny. Well, I can say that, pessimistic as to human destiny, I am optimistic as to man.'

[2] p. 74. 'I continue to believe that this world has no ultimate meaning. But I know that something in it has meaning and that is man, because he is the only creature to insist on having one. This world has at least the truth of man and our task is to provide its justifications against fate itself. And it has no justification but man; hence he must be saved if we want to save the idea we have of life. With your scornful smile you will ask me: what do you mean by saving men? And with all my being I shout to you that I mean not mutilating him and yet giving a chance to the justice which man alone can conceive.'

Dr Rieux announces that his only aim in life is 'to be a man', and one knows that he considers this the highest goal a man can attain. Later, he talks of 'ceux qui se suffisent de l'homme' with undisguised admiration. The spectacle of a man like Rieux, fighting against all odds to affirm the dignity of the human presence, is one to excite Camus's most profound love. Like all great passions, this love is founded on instinct rather than reason. If reason were brought to bear, Camus could not assert, as he does in *La Peste*, that men were only guilty through ignorance. He could not claim that all men were essentially innocent, in direct opposition to the Christian dogma that all men are essentially guilty. Reason would show that both positions are extreme and untenable. When passion has subsided, Camus remains a convinced humanist (with a small 'h') who always assumes that a person is good and decent until it is proven otherwise. He sees more to admire in men than to despise – 'il y a dans les hommes plus de choses à admirer que de choses à mépriser'.[1] *La Peste* shows that if men approach each other in this spirit, they will discover the intense pleasure of solidarity that is experienced by Rieux, Tarrou, Rambert, Grand, in their struggle against the enemy which threatens their common humanity. The plague is the 'affaire de tous', everyone is in it together, therefore they look for what unites them; Rieux tries hard to concentrate on what he has in common with Paneloux, and exemplifies better than the priest the commandment that one should love one's neighbour as oneself. Only, the self-sacrifice shown by Rieux, Tarrou, Rambert, Grand, Kaliayev (in *Les Justes*), is not accompanied by prayer, nor does it expect a reward. It is motivated by a simple, selfless respect for man, whose nobility is demonstrated in the very courage he displays every day, as he perseveres with a life which can never have meaning. Hence Camus's constant respect for others, for their views, their beliefs, their fears and their failings. They are united in sharing the same absurd destiny. 'Je voulais seulement que les hommes retrouvent leur

[1] p. 331. 'there are more things to admire in men than to despise.'

solidarité pour entrer en lutte contre leur destin révoltant.'[1]

Camus's love of man is finally expressed in the many pages which testify to a real and profound compassion for the vulnerability and loneliness of men, separated from the love of their fellows either by exile (Rambert, Rieux), old age (Grand, and the old people of *L'Envers et L'Endroit*), inability to make contact (Cottard), inability to express themselves (Grand, Camus's mother), poverty, or death. The deaths of the Othon child and of Tarrou are described by a man of real sensitivity. Tarrou and Rieux, though associates, do not manage to declare their love and respect for each other before Tarrou's moving death. Camus knew that a declaration of love was never adequate to its task, and that people were always passing each other, as strangers, for want of the ability, or the courage, to say that they loved. ('Un amour n'est jamais assez fort pour trouver sa propre expression.'[2]) If the ability or the courage were eventually to be harnessed, often it would be too late, or it would be misinterpreted. In *La Mort Heureuse* Camus had written, 'par quel paradoxe cruel nous nous trompons toujours deux fois sur les êtres que nous aimons, à leur bénéfice d'abord et à leur désavantage ensuite'.[3] When all is said and done, Camus was first and foremost the spokesman of such people, whose lives were ended without really having begun.

* * *

Allegory

It is time to approach the matter of *La Peste*'s allegorical significance. That it is not fanciful to perceive allegorical meaning is attested by various hints in the text (plagues are a 'chose commune', the pestilence was the 'affaire de tous', etc.), and by a note of Camus's in his *Carnets*:

---

[1] *Lettres à un Ami Allemand*, p. 73. 'I merely wanted men to rediscover their solidarity in order to wage war against their revolting fate.'

[2] p. 313. 'love is never strong enough to find the words befitting it.'

[3] p. 165. 'by what cruel paradox we twice deceive ourselves about those whom we love, to their advantage the first time, and then to their detriment.' (BM)

> Je veux exprimer au moyen de la peste l'étouffement dont
> nous avons tous souffert et l'atmosphère de menace et
> d'exil dans laquelle nous avons vécu. Je veux du même
> coup étendre cette interprétation à la notion d'existence
> en général.[1]

There is, then, a literal interpretation, of a city beleaguered
by plague, and several metaphorical ones, which frequently
overlap and vie for precedence in the grand scheme. For this
reason, it is perhaps better to call *La Peste* a 'symbolic' novel,
rather than an allegory, since the allegory is intermittent, not
constant. Indeed, there is a profusion of symbols, open to a
profusion of interpretations.[2]

The first, most obvious, and finally least satisfactory interpretation presents the plague as a symbol of the Occupation.
There can be no doubt that Camus intended his book to be a
tribute to his colleagues in the Resistance and a powerful
image of what it was like to live under the rule of totalitarian
occupation forces. This is what he means by 'atmosphère de
menance et d'exil' in the note mentioned above, and in the
letter to Roland Barthes (11 January 1955) he states explicitly
his intention to depict resistance against Nazism.[3] The parallels
are striking. Rieux, Tarrou, Rambert and Grand are Resistance
fighters. Cottard is the collaborator. Paneloux's sermons
represent the attitude of the Church, which did in fact tell
Frenchmen that the German invasion was a punishment for
their sins,[4] Paneloux himself could be a tribute to the many
courageous Christians with whom Camus fought; the gates of
Oran are closed and communications with the outside world
suspended, as France was so treated by division. A curfew
is imposed. Food is rationed, electricity becomes scarce, and
police are more in evidence on the streets. When the plague

[1] 'I wish to express through the plague the suffocation which we have all
suffered and the atmosphere of threat and exile in which we have lived.
At the same time I want to extend this interpretation to the notion of
existence in general.' (BM)

[2] John Cruickshank, op. cit., p. 167.

[3] *Pléiade* edition, p. 1965.

[4] Philip Thody, op. cit., p. 99.

subsides, there are celebrations, similar to the celebrations which welcomed the Liberation of Paris. Cottard, the collaborator, is hunted down and murdered. The weakness of the analogy is apparent, however, when we remember that war is a result of the wickedness of men towards men, whereas a plague is a natural catastrophe for which men have no responsibility. There is no solid comparison possible between the impersonal cruelty of an epidemic, and the *human* cruelty of the Occupation forces. In Camus's mind, however, the comparison might carry some weight, given his reluctance to recognize that men could be *inherently* cruel.

On the metaphorical level, the plague represents the face of death, in its most extreme, capricious and arbitrary form. It is 'un interminable piétinement qui écrasait tout sur son passage'.[1] It forces the inhabitants to admit, for the first time perhaps, their mortality, and to draw the consequences from this realization. It must be admitted that, in this regard, the symbolism is totally successful. There can be no image more horrific than imprisonment of a whole population slowly decimated by a pestilence which might mean death for any one of them within hours. In such circumstances, one would be bound to reflect. By extension, the plague represents anything which, like death, negates human effort or poisons the joy of living. It is frequently referred to as an 'abstraction', at which times it stands for all that passes the comprehension of men and threatens their happiness. And what is this alienation between men and the world but the 'Absurd' described in *Le Mythe de Sisyphe*? The plague itself does not directly represent the Absurd, but the extreme circumstances it entails provokes the inhabitants of Oran to an *experience* of the Absurd by confronting them, unexpectedly, with death. On this level, too, the symbolism works so well that even the reader is forced to undergo a *pseudo*-experience of the Absurd. This is only another way of saying that the plague forces its victims to come to terms with the condition of life, not in any superficial

[1] p. 198. 'The slow, deliberate progress of some monstrous thing crushing out all upon its path.'

intellectual way, but fundamentally. The old asthmatic patient, who hardly appears in the novel, says, 'Mais qu'est-ce que ça veut dire, la peste? C'est la vie, et voilà tout.'[1]

A curious interpretation has been advanced in a much-acclaimed book by a psycho-analyst[2] according to which the plague represents the silence of Camus's mother, and Rieux's struggle is no less than Camus's long fight against sexual inhibition, occasioned by his mother. If this strikes you as odd, there is much that is odder in the same book. Meursault, firing two shots at the Arab he murders in *L'Etranger*, thus dispenses with both his father and mother (p. 74). In having no legs, Zagreus in *La Mort Heureuse* symbolizes double castration (p. 60). Most astonishing of all, the struggle of Sisyphus to push his heavy load to the top of the hill represents the effort of the child in defecating, and it has to be repeated because the mother is never satisfied with the visible results of that effort (p. 112). There is much more in this book to delight the psycho-analyst.

Finally, there is an interior as well as an exterior infection represented by the plague. This is the power of evil which can take possession of the human heart and make men enter into complicity with the 'exterior' plague. 'Cette cochonnerie de maladie! Même ceux qui ne l'ont pas la portent dans leur cœur.'[3] This interior infection gives rise to duplicity, lies, deceit, selfishness, all the ways in which a man may be contaminated and tricked into complicity with a world based on injustice. This is what Tarrou means when he says, 'je souffrais déjà de la peste bien avant de connaître cette ville et cette épidémie'.[4] An interpretation which leans towards the plague as an evil which we all carry within us makes the analogy with the Occupation more plausible. For, by suggesting that there is an inner taint

[1] p. 330. 'But what does that mean – "plague"? Just life, no more than that.'

[2] Alain Costes, *Albert Camus ou La Parole Manquante* (1973).

[3] p. 131. 'This bloody disease! Even those that haven't caught it carry it around in their hearts.' (BM)

[4] p. 266. 'I had plague already, long before I came to this town and encountered it here.'

which corresponds to the cosmic disaster of the plague, and which works in collusion with it, the actions of the Occupation forces are more explicable. The analogy is not developed, however, to this degree. Tarrou is the only character to refer to an 'inner plague', and he means by this not so much a source of evil as a lack of resolve to combat evil, or conscious failure to do so efficiently. To revolt against the plague means to deny any temptation to add to the misfortunes of men and to comfort them in the miseries which befall them.

La Peste was written during the Second World War, and is a product of that war. It is written with passion and pain. Nothing, Camus says, nothing will ever justify the weight of suffering inflicted upon men, and any ideology, religion or idea which attempts to do so must be resisted. *La Peste* is an attack on abstract intellectualism. It is a plea for a halt to the assumed position, the empty talk, the theoretic compassion, the laboured 'points of view', a plea for living, in spite of or even because it is the most difficult enterprise in the world.

*   *   *

Les Justes

Camus gave up the editorship of *Combat* soon after the Liberation but continued to write the occasional article on political issues. His creative work now reverted to the theatre, with *L'Etat de Siège* (1948) and *Les Justes* (1950).

L'Etat de Siège was a mistake. There are many people still alive who saw the Jean-Louis Barrault production in 1948 and shudder with the memory. To read it now, it is difficult to see how it could work. The language is stilted, unnatural; the conception is epic; declamatory speeches which abound in just the sort of abstract nonsense which Camus detested are met with rejoinders of staggering banality. The play is meant to be an attack on all forms of dictatorship; it deplores tyranny and nihilism alike, and its central character, Diego, is a hero of Revolt who refuses to side with the gods against men.

Les Justes, on the other hand, though written very quickly, is perhaps Camus's best play. It is based on the true story of a small group of revolutionaries in Russia in 1905, the 'scrupulous assassins' as Camus calls them (*meurtriers délicats*). The action of the play centres around the conflict of ideals between two of the group, Stepan and Kaliayev. Stepan is an orthodox revolutionary who believes that the ends justify the means, whatever they are. He affirms that he is ready to kill children indiscriminately and deliberately if it will advance the cause of revolution. No action is 'wrong', he says, if it contributes to the eventual reign of justice on the earth. Stepan is a nihilist, who has himself suffered at the hands of official justice and spent a period in prison, and is now motivated by a desire for revenge. He is a dupe to the 'abstractions' which so often seduce a man away from his better self, and which was one of the obsessions of Camus. Kaliayev tells Stepan that he entered the revolution because he loved life. Stepan's reply is: 'Je n'aime pas la vie, mais la justice qui est au-dessus de la vie.'[1] It is Camus's contention that Stepan is doubly wrong, (*a*) because nothing has a higher value than human life, (*b*) because justice is merely an idea to him, not an event in the lives of people.

Kaliayev (who keeps his historical name) is quite the opposite. Where Stepan strives for a postulated but uncertain future, Kaliayev acts for the present; he refuses to sacrifice people who are alive now for people who may be alive tomorrow. Where Stepan is motivated by hatred, Kaliayev is motivated by love. Where Stepan is unscrupulous, Kaliayev refuses to compromise the honour and dignity of men:

> Mais moi, j'aime ceux qui vivent aujourd'hui sur la même terre que moi, et c'est eux que je salue. C'est pour eux que je lutte et que je consens à mourir. Et pour une cité lointaine, dont je ne suis pas sûr, je n'irai pas frapper le visage de mes frères. Je n'irai pas ajouter à l'injustice vivante pour une justice morte . . . si un jour, moi vivant, la révolution devait se séparer de l'honneur, je m'en détournerais.[2]

[1] Act 1, p. 46. 'I do not love life; I love something higher – and that is justice.'

[2] Act 2, p. 62. 'But those *I* love are the men who are alive today, and

Kaliayev's function in the revolution is to assassinate the Grand Duke. (A distinction is made here between murder and assassination.) He will throw a bomb into the Duke's carriage as it passes. He will do it, because it is necessary, but at the same time he shrinks in horror from the act and knows it is, in any circumstances, difficult to justify. When the time comes, however, the Grand Duke is unexpectedly accompanied by his little niece and nephew. Kaliayev cannot go through with the assassination: 'Ces deux petits visages sérieux et dans ma main, ce poids terrible. C'est sur eux qu'il fallait le lancer. Ainsi. Tout droit. Oh, non! Je n'ai pas pu.'[1] Tarrou in *La Peste* announced that he aimed to be a 'saint without God', to remain innocent in spite of the dangers of fighting injustice. This is approximately Kaliayev's ideal also. 'J'ai choisi d'être innocent', he says, and, when he returns to the act and does finally kill the Grand Duke, unaccompanied this time by the children, Kaliayev will not consider himself guilty. In his view, he has expunged a revolting political idea, not killed a man. The situation has a sharp irony when the Grand Duchess visits Kaliayev in prison after the crime and confronts him with the human reality of his deed. The Grand Duke, this 'political idea', was an absent-minded and somnolent old man, who spoke of justice just as Kaliayev now does, and whose niece and nephew, still alive, are not such angels. Tarrou's ideal of innocence is still impossible, it seems.

Nevertheless, *Les Justes* proposes for the first time a concept which is elaborated in *L'Homme Révolté*, that of *la mesure* – moderation. Revolt must be restricted by respect for man. There are *limits* to be observed, and not everything is permitted.

---

walk this same earth. It's they whom I hail, it is for them I am fighting, for them I am ready to lay down my life. But I shall not strike my brothers in the face for the sake of some far-off city, which, for all I know, may not exist. I refuse to add to the living injustice all round me for the sake of a dead justice . . . if one day the revolution thinks fit to break with honour, well, I'm through with the revolution.'

[1] Act 2, p. 57. 'Those two serious little faces, and in my hand that hideous weight. I'd have to throw it at *them*. Like that! Straight at them. No, I just couldn't bring myself.'

'Même dans la destruction, il y a un ordre, il y a des limites',[1] says Dora, who further maintains that a revolution which offends morality, which has no scruples, and which commits present atrocities in the name of a future which its victims will not live to see, will be bound to lose the support of the people, and rightly so. The point is brought out in the following exchange:

> DORA: Ouvre les yeux et comprends que l'Organisation perdrait ses pouvoirs et son influence si elle tolérait, un seul moment, que des enfants fussent broyés par nos bombes.
> STEPAN: Je n'ai pas assez de cœur pour ces niaiseries. Quand nous nous déciderons à oublier les enfants, ce jour-là, nous serons les maîtres du monde et la révolution triomphera.
> DORA: Ce jour-là, la révolution sera haïe de l'humanité entière.[2]

Stepan regards these scruples as luxuries of the bourgeois class. Many of Camus's critics agreed with him. How will anything ever be achieved by such mealy-mouthed middle-class boy-scouts as Kaliayev, they cried. The severe criticism to which Camus was subjected after the publication of *L'Homme Révolté*, really started in the theatre in 1950. His celebration of the 'scrupulous assassins' was a disappointment to some of his more rampant Socialist followers who looked to him for the leadership of a New Society, and found instead the portrait of a man with a delicate moral conscience. Kaliayev's moral

[1] Act 2, p. 61. 'Even in destruction there's a right way and a wrong way – and there are limits.'

[2] Act 2, p. 59.

DORA: Open your eyes, Stepan, and try to realize that the group would lose all its driving force, were it to tolerate, even for a moment, the idea of children's being blown to pieces by your bombs.

STEPAN: Sorry, but I don't suffer from a tender heart; that sort of nonsense cuts no ice with *me*. . . . Not until the day comes when we stop sentimentalizing about children will the revolution triumph, and we be masters of the world.

DORA: When that day comes, the revolution will be loathed by the whole human race.

position confronts him with a dilemma which he can only resolve by suicide. Since he accepts the proposition that to take human life is inexcusable, but to take the life of the Grand Duke is necessary, the only way in which he can reconcile these apparently contradictory imperatives is to pay with his own life. Suicide is then seen as a redemption. It would be wrong to castigate Camus for what seems a denial of one of his most cherished precepts, that suicide is not a valid response to the injustice of life (*Le Mythe de Sisyphe*). This is suicide of quite a different sort. Kaliayev is not killing himself as a protest against injustice, but as an expiation for his having had, unavoidably, to contribute to that injustice. However, it is a questionable ethic. His death cannot undo the death of the Grand Duke. And Communists were quick to point out that progress would be impossible if every revolutionary who exterminated a tyrant had to kill himself.

What makes the story individual to Camus is the persistent doubt that troubles these benevolent assassins. They are not sure of themselves. They wonder about the contradictions inherent in their position and they do not know all the answers. No one else could have written *Les Justes* from quite that point of view.

5

L'Homme Révolté

L'Homme Révolté examines in greater detail the preoccupation at the basis of *Les Justes,* namely, is the taking of human life ever justified, even in the pursuit of a revolt which will improve the lot of human beings? This essay marks the culminating point in a natural evolution of thought: *L'Etranger* and *Le Mythe de Sisyphe* established a personal ethic; *La Peste* applied that ethic to communal relations; *L'Homme Révolté* attempts to apply it even further, to politics, which is the study of ethics in society. Camus wants to know how it is possible for governments to murder masses of ordinary folk in the name of policies which proclaim the rights of the people. What has gone wrong?

Camus states the problem, at the beginning, by resuming the avowed preoccupation of both Tarrou and Kaliayev: 'Il s'agit de savoir si l'innocence, à partir du moment où elle agit, ne peut s'empêcher de tuer'.[1] To decide, he reverts to the principles of *Le Mythe de Sisyphe.* The Absurd invalidates all prejudice, all preconceived notions, all transcendental values. The world is ridiculous and senseless. Therefore all human acts are equal, and equally useless. Vice and virtue are the result of accident, and of indifferent value. But one initial value did arise from a contemplation of the Absurd, and that was the rejection of suicide, on the grounds that the Absurd can only be maintained by a preservation of the human presence which challenges it: 'le rejet du suicide et le maintien de cette con-

[1] p. 14. 'It is a question of finding out whether innocence, the moment it begins to act, can avoid committing murder.'

frontation désespérée entre l'interrogation humaine et le silence du monde.'[1] Well, if suicide is inadmissible, it presupposes that human life is recognized as the only necessary and precious value; it follows from that that the extinction of someone else's life is equally as 'wrong' as the extinction of one's own, 'meurtre et suicide sont une même chose, qu'il faut prendre ou rejeter ensemble'.[2] Hence murder is not permissible in the 'absurd' world.

The logic of this reasoning is very suspect. In the first place, Camus does not say (either here or in *Le Mythe de Sisyphe*) why it is so important to maintain the confrontation between an unjust world and the individual conscience which perceives it to be unjust. Logically, there can be no objection to suicide which would indeed remove the problem. But if it is 'important' that the problem be maintained, then Camus is using an adjective which can only be based on an *a priori* value judgement. It is quite clear that he feels, instinctively, that human life is the ultimate value, but this decision does not arise from a rejection of suicide; rather, it must logically precede that rejection, since any investigation into the merits or otherwise of suicide implies that there is some value attached to the life which is to be taken. Then, having declared that suicide is invalid, it is by no means a logical step to conclude that murder is invalid by extension or analogy. Camus is making a moral distinction, no other. By the value which he places on human life, Camus is fundamentally as much a transcendentalist as the bourgeois moralists he professes to dislike.

Be that as it may, Camus proceeds to demonstrate how revolt has been misconceived in history. Most revolutions, he says, have been founded on murder, whereas true revolt is a protest against death, the ultimate injustice in the human condition. 'La conséquence de la révolte, au contraire, est de refuser sa légitimation au meurtre puisque dans son principe, elle est

---

[1] p. 16. 'the rejection of suicide and persistence in that hopeless encounter between human questioning and the silence of the universe.'

[2] p. 17. 'Murder and suicide are the same thing; one must accept them both or reject them both.'

protestation contre la mort.'[1] He gives manifold examples which it would be laborious to enumerate in detail. Revolt is betrayed, in the first place, by nihilism. The example he gives to illustrate this point is a fictional one – Ivan Karamazov.[2] Karamazov maintains that, since God does not exist, everything is permissible, and deduces from this intuition (with far more logic than Camus) that there is no positive value in preserving life rather than extinguishing it. Nihilistic revolt, as we know, leads to insanity. Then there is de Sade, whose mistake was to pursue the absolute, which led him to indulge his own desires at the expense of other people and thus betray one of the tenets of revolt – the respect for the dignity of all men. (We have come a long way since Don Juan, the precursor of de Sade, who was put forward in *Le Mythe de Sisyphe* as one of the heroes of the absurdist ethic; *La Peste* and the Second World War have intervened between the two essays.) Camus then examines the influence of Hegel on revolt, and concludes that he sacrificed revolt for people in favour of a prophetic revolt for an idea, and that this pernicious influence continues to be felt in modern Communism. The error lies in promising Nirvana instead of improving life as it is.

From the very beginning, Camus's work has testified to a profound distrust of any absolute doctrine which, in its blind evangelism, neglects the living persons for whose benefit it was originally formulated. He does not like enthusiastic intellectual plans. He does not respect the ideas of men, but men themselves. In *L'Homme Révolté* he says, 'On exige que soit considéré ce qui, dans l'homme, ne peut se réduire à l'idée, cette part chaleureuse qui ne peut servir à rien d'autre qu'à être',[3] and in an article for *Combat* reprinted in *Actuelles I*,

---

[1] p. 342. 'The consequence of rebellion, on the contrary, is to refuse to legitimize murder because rebellion, in principle, is a protest against death.'

[2] See *The Brothers Karamazov* by F. Dostoievsky.

[3] p. 32. 'We demand that that part of man which cannot be confined to the realm of ideas should be taken into consideration – the passionate side of his nature that serves no other purpose but to help him to live.'

he says, 'Quand on veut unifier le monde entier au nom d'une théorie, il n'est pas d'autres voies que de rendre ce monde aussi décharné, aveugle et sourd que la théorie elle-même'.[1] The *leitmotiv* of this collection of articles is an unequivocal condemnation of terrifying abstract doctrines which have, in history, mutilated so many men. This applies to doctrines founded on formal morality and to those founded on the absence of all morality.

Camus does not consider his version of revolt to be abstract or destructive, because it never treats man as an historical statistic. On the contrary, it creates new values, or rather reveals and re-asserts values which are in danger of being submerged. The discovery of the Absurd, remember, is made by a consciousness which recognizes the world to be unjust. To do so, it must be aware, at the same time, of a concept of 'justice' which the world does not measure up to. Where does it find this concept but within itself, or within man? So revolt does not only refuse the world, it proclaims the values in man which are lacking in the world. It is thus creative, constructive, and affirmative. It affirms some intangible human 'worth' to which the Absurd is an insult. The first value revealed by the position of revolt is something approaching a human nature. Camus does call it human nature at one point (p. 28), but to avoid ambiguity I shall call it the integrity of the human presence. This is quite definitely a value judgement, and Camus recognizes it as such: 'nous trouvons un jugement de valeur au nom duquel le révolté refuse son approbation à la condition qui est la sienne.'[2]

Now this 'integrity' is not unique to the individual consciousness which perceives it, but common to all men. Thus the second value is revealed by the position of revolt – human fraternity and solidarity: 'Dans la révolte, l'homme se dépasse en autrui

---

[1] p. 260. 'If you want to unify the entire world in the name of a theory, the only way you will do so is to make the world as gaunt, as blind, and as deaf as the theory itself.' (BM)

[2] p. 39. 'we find an assessment of values in the name of which the rebel refuses to accept the condition in which he finds himself.'

et, de ce point de vue, la solidarité humaine est métaphysique
. . . Le révolté lutte pour l'intégrité d'une partie de son être . . .
il se borne à refuser l'humiliation, sans la demander pour
l'autre.'[1] The act of revolt is epitomized for Camus in the
relationship between slave and master. When the slave eventually says 'no' to a specific order, he speaks in the name of an inviolable human worth which the master threatens to humiliate.

Revolt engenders the love of all 'slaves' for each other in an
united struggle against their common destiny. Camus is not so
naïve as to suggest that all men are alike (see *Actuelles*, p. 130),
but he does contend that what unites him to men with different
ethnic or cultural backgrounds is more important than what
divides him from them, and that he cannot deny this common
humanity without, by implication, degrading himself. The
evolution in thought from the individual experience of the
Absurd to the collective experience of Revolt (from *Le Mythe
de Sisyphe* to *L'Homme Révolté*) is clear. Camus puts it this
way: 'Dans l'expérience absurde, la souffrance est individuelle.
A partir du mouvement de révolte, elle a conscience d'être
collective, elle est l'aventure de tous.'[2] As Rambert discovers in
La Peste, the pestilence is everyone's business, 'l'affaire de
tous'.

What, then, has gone wrong? Why have revolutions consistently betrayed the principles of revolt? The answer lies in
the fact that, as soon as the principle of revolt is translated into
political action, it must inevitably compromise itself. Or so it
has invariably done in the past. In order to obtain justice for
the slaves, one must deny justice to the masters. The choice is a
cruel one. The rebel cannot condone injustice, yet in refusing
to do so, he is likely to commit injustice. 'Le révolté ne peut

---

[1] pp. 29–31. 'When he rebels, a man identifies himself with other men and,
from this point of view, human solidarity is metaphysical. . . . He is fighting
for the integrity of one part of his being . . . the rebel, on principle, per-
sistently refuses to be humiliated without asking that others should be.'

[2] p. 35. 'In absurdist experience, suffering is individual. But from the
moment that a movement of rebellion begins, suffering is seen as a collective
experience – as the experience of everyone.'

donc trouver le repos. Il sait le bien et fait malgré lui le mal.'[1]
The brotherhood which is a guiding principle of revolt cannot,
in the nature of things, extend to a brotherhood between slave
and master. Camus seems here to come up against a very
serious stumbling-block in the practical application of his
theory. For theory it is, and therein lies the fault of *L'Homme
Révolté*. In *Le Mythe de Sisyphe* Camus presented a magnifi-
cently clear description of an intuition, and in *La Peste* he gave
a fictional representation of it. Now he is attempting to explain
the inconsistencies and contradictions which are uncovered
when he carries his intuition into the political arena. Camus is
not a successful theoretician, and does not explain satisfactorily.
(Conor Cruise O'Brien has recently claimed that Camus resolves the conflict by condemning revolutionary violence and
conniving at political violence which is used to defend the
status quo, but this is mischievous, unfair, and blatantly
untrue.[2])

Camus now argues that most revolutionary movements have
failed to reflect genuine revolt because they have not been
moderate. Camus borrows the principle of moderation (*la
mesure*), the third to evolve from the position of revolt, from
the Greeks, for whom he had had a predilection since his
university days, when he had written a comparative thesis on
Plotinus and Saint Augustin. Adèle King has very clearly
shown the influence of the Greek ideal of order and harmony
upon Camus's thought, and concludes that his form of revolt
is 'a rather uneasy synthesis between a Greek ideal and a
Nordic discontent'.[3] In an essay roughly contemporary in
conception with *L'Homme Révolté* and subsequently published
in *Eté*, Camus writes: 'Les Grecs qui se sont interrogés pendant
des siècles sur ce qui est juste ne pourraient rien comprendre à
notre idée de la justice. L'équité, pour eux, supposait une limite
tandis que tout notre continent se convulse à la recherche d'une

---

[1] p. 342. 'Thus the rebel can never find peace. He knows what is good
and, despite himself, does evil.'
[2] Conor Cruise O'Brien, op. cit., p. 59.
[3] Adéle King, *Camus*, p. 40.

justice qu'il veut totale.'[1] The Greek value of moderation, then, should be the guiding principle of revolt. The slave rebels against the master because he has gone beyond a certain *limit*; the slave therefore knows the importance of limits, and his rebellion is provoked because they have been infringed. He must keep in mind the importance he attaches to limits both during and after his rebellion, for he, of all people, should respect them. This is a fair description of the state of mind of a Kaliayev, for example. The limit which the rebel must impose upon himself is set by an awareness of the first value derived from revolt – a respect for the supreme integrity of individual human life. Viewed in this way, revolt is not exclusively negative. It does not only refuse to tolerate a situation, but in so doing affirms values of its own – dignity, solidarity, and moderation. It must never forget that its ultimate aim is also a positive one – the establishment of a greater degree of human happiness. As long as the rebel bears in mind the ideal of moderation, he stands a chance of achieving this aim, for he realizes that he is fighting for the maintenance of relativity in human affairs. A greater degree of happiness, yes, a greater degree of justice, yes, a greater degree of freedom, yes, but not total happiness, absolute justice, or absolute freedom, all of which are inaccessible and impossible, and which poison man's effort. The rebel is striving for a relative, limited justice, because he is free of the dogma which claims to justify absolutes. The rebel is therefore something of a realist: 'il faut une part de réalisme à toute morale', writes Camus, 'la vertu toute pure est meurtrière; et qu'il faut une part de morale à tout réalisme; le cynisme est meurtrier.'[2] And in *Actuelles I* we find, 'je plaide pour un vrai réalisme contre une mythologie à la fois illogique

---

[1] *Eté*, p. 134. 'The Greeks, who spent centuries asking themselves what was just, would understand nothing of our idea of justice. Equity, for them, supposed a limit, while our whole continent is convulsed by the quest for a justice which it sees as absolute.'

[2] p. 355. 'at least one part of realism is necessary to every ethic: unadulterated virtue, pure and simple, is homicidal. On the other hand, there must be a part of ethics in all realism, for pure cynicism can also be murderous.' (BM)

et meurtrière et contre le nihilisme romantique, qu'il soit bourgeois ou prétenduement révolutionnaire'.[1] It is a realism which recognizes the basic fact that absolute justice must lamentably but inevitably conflict with personal liberty. Therefore a degree of justice and a degree of liberty are all that one may hope to attain, and thereby achieve a fine balance and harmony which respects both. Those who aim higher are deluded by the belief in the perfectibility of man, an absolute like any other. No, he is not perfect, though he is, on balance, more admirable than despicable (see *La Peste*), but given the intoxication of a doctrinaire philosophy based on the pursuit of absolutes, the slave risks becoming the master and neglecting, in turn, the respect for limits which led him to rebel in the first place. If the rebel can remember the larger application of his action, that of man against an irrational universe, he will perhaps even achieve the most elusive objective of all in the modern world, the brotherhood of slave and master united against a common disgrace. This alone would be sufficient to rescue him from the lure of absolutism. Here, then, is how Camus sees the principle of *mesure*:

> . . . la liberté la plus extrême, celle de tuer, n'est pas compatible avec les raisons de la révolte. La révolte n'est nullement une revendication de liberté totale. Au contraire, la révolte fait le procès de la liberté totale. Elle conteste justement le pouvoir illimité qui autorise un supérieur à violer la frontière interdite. Loin de revendiquer une indépendance générale, le révolté veut qu'il soit reconnu que la liberté a ses limites partout où se trouve un être humain, la limite étant précisément le pouvoir de révolte de cet être. . . . Le révolté exige sans doute une certaine liberté pour lui-même; mais en aucun cas, s'il est conséquent, le droit de détruire l'être et la liberté de l'autre. Il n'humilie personne. La liberté qu'il réclame, il la revenique pour tous; celle qu'il refuse, il l'interdit à tous. Il n'est pas seulement esclave contre maître, mais aussi homme contre le monde du maître et de l'esclave. . . .

---

[1] 'I plead for a genuine realism against a mythology which is both illogical and murderous, and against romantic nihilism, whether it be middle-class or so-called revolutionary.' (BM)

C'est au nom d'une autre valeur que le révolté affirme l'impossibilité de la liberté totale en même temps qu'il réclame pour lui-même la relative liberté, nécessaire pour reconnaître cette impossibilité. Chaque liberté humaine, à sa racine la plus profonde, est ainsi relative.[1]

*　　　*　　　*

The Quarrel with Sartre

It was inevitable that Camus's recommendation of limited revolt should appear tepid to the left wing, which had all but canonized him and now felt cheated by its hero. The public argument which followed the publication of *L'Homme Révolté* was the kind of knockabout quarrel in which French intellectuals occasionally indulge, and it was led by Jean-Paul Sartre, through his friend and disciple Francis Jeanson. Sartre and Camus had for long been coupled in the public mind, with some reason. They were both preoccupied with the vulnerability of man in a meaningless world, they both claimed that it was nevertheless possible to create a purposeful life, they were both atheists and humanists, they both rejected established moral codes. They did not meet until 1944. Politically, they co-operated to some extent until about 1948, finding themselves on the same side, for instance, against Fascist Spain and against

[1] p. 341. 'the most extreme form of freedom, the freedom to kill, is not compatible with the motives of rebellion. Rebellion is in no way the demand for total freedom. On the contrary, rebellion puts total freedom up for trial. The object of its attack is exactly the unlimited power which authorizes a superior to violate the forbidden frontier. Far from demanding general independence, the rebel wants it to be recognised that freedom has its limits everywhere that a human being is to be found – the limit being precisely that human being's power to rebel. . . . The rebel demands undoubtedly a certain degree of freedom for himself; but in no case, if he is consistent, does he demand the right to destroy the existence and the freedom of others. He humiliates no one. The freedom he claims, he claims for all; the freedom he refuses, he forbids everyone to enjoy. He is not only the slave against the master, but also man against the world of master and slave. . . . It is in the name of another value that the rebel affirms the impossibility of total freedom while he claims for himself the relative freedom necessary to recognize this impossibility. Every human freedom, at its very roots, is therefore relative.'

Western imperialism. For a short time Camus was sympathetic towards Sartre's left-wing non-Communist party, although he never joined it. But it was always an uneasy alliance, because Sartre was the acknowledged apostle of existentialism, and Camus was unequivocally opposed to it. In *Le Mythe de Sisyphe* he defined existentialism as philosophic suicide (p. 62), and in *Nouvelles Littéraires* (15 November 1945) he pointed out that the book had been specifically directed against the existentialist view. The confusion arose largely because the term 'existential' had been vulgarized to such an extent that it came to encompass anyone who held that the world left something to be desired. As Camus said, 80 per cent of the people whose conversation he heard on the Métro were existential by this definition. Basically, the difference between Sartre and Camus was that Sartre denied the existence of a 'human nature', while Camus upheld it. For Sartre, man could not be defined in advance by any adjective, there was no human nature, or 'essence' which he could fall back on; he defined himself *a posteriori* by his acts. For Camus, on the other hand, a man's acts could reveal an intrinsic integrity or dignity which were always there, but which had lain dormant and unasserted until he was made to face the absurdity of his mortal condition in an immortal universe. This is tantamount to saying that there are, after all, certain *a priori* values. Take justice, for instance; Sartre would say that there is no such thing, that this is a meaningless word, and the acts of men cannot be measured in this way according to a nebulous, pre-existing, non-human criterion. Camus says that men act in accordance with a sense of justice which is innate, and which is of human origin, since they are alone in the world to conceive it. Camus's attitude does suggest a certain spirituality which is totally absent from Sartre's scheme of things. It is not altogether surprising that Sartre should find in *L'Homme Révolté* a disguised defence of transcendental values.

In the summer of 1952 there appeared a bitter review of *L'Homme Révolté* in Sartre's review *Temps Modernes*. It was signed by Francis Jeanson. Three months later, Camus published in the same review a long reply to Sartre, which was in turn answered by both Sartre and Jeanson. Some of the language used was quite insulting. The existentialist thinkers found the mild liberalism of *L'Homme Révolté* aloof and priggish; they said Camus was little more than a benevolent distributor of alms; they went so far as to imply that he was a lackey of imperialism (a view recently resurrected by Dr O'Brien). Camus, it must be said, never once insulted his critics, though presumably they would not be surprised by this further evidence of lack of vigour on his part. More seriously, they accused him of being a moralist, and this requires some investigation.

When dealing with *L'Etranger* I have said that Camus was a moralist only in the Molièresque sense, that he brought the reader's attention to certain behaviour, commented upon it, but abstained from preaching lessons that should be drawn from it. In *L'Homme Révolté* he has become a moralist in the sense that he does recommend how we ought to live. If he has not actually mounted a pulpit, he has at least procured a pedestal. This is what Sartre and Jeanson found so objectionable. Their own ethical attitude was constantly evolving, infinitely pragmatic, and they saw in *L'Homme Révolté* a regenerate reliance on moral values which were hopelessly static.

Furthermore, one of the principles to which the existentialists were most devoted was the idea of commitment (*l'engagement*). Now, Camus's career had been eloquent testimony of his own commitment, both during and after the war, but he had never actually used the word as a battle-cry in the way that Sartre had. In 1946, he had written that he had no time for *la littérature engagée*: 'il paraît qu'écrire aujourd'hui un poème sur le printemps serait servir le capitalisme. . . . Oui, je les souhaiterais moins engagés dans leurs œuvres et un peu plus dans leur vie de chaque jour.'[1] Sartre could find no

---

[1] 'it seems today that to write a poem on springtime would be to serve capitalism. . . . I should rather they were less committed in their writings and slightly more so in their everyday life.' *Carnets* (BM)

evidence of commitment in *L'Homme Révolté*. Its recommendation of non-violent revolt was so vague that one could not see
what there was to be committed to. It is true that Camus pays
little attention to the potential practical application of his
proposals. Their most serious fault, for a Marxist existentialist,
was that they were ineffective. Sartre held more or less to the
Marxist view that action must be effective before all else, and
that therefore the ends justify the means. Camus's concern
that the means should not themselves be harmful ('Il est des
moyens qui ne s'excusent pas', wrote Camus in *Lettres à un
Ami Allemand*[1]), coupled with his principle of moderation,
would totally emasculate his revolt. From this point of view,
the debate between Sartre and Camus mirrors the dialogue
between Stepan and Kaliayev in *Les Justes*.

In the end, the two men could not easily be reconciled because their fundamental attitudes were so sharply divided.
Hence Sartre accused Camus of operating a double standard,
of criticizing Marxist revolutions and being silent on the
matter of US imperialism, while Camus thought that Sartre
was unduly harsh on America and turned a blind eye to the
transgressions of Russia. Yet they both indubitably had a
social conscience, and of the two, I think Camus was the more
impartial. It is simply not true to say that he was reactionary,
or that he connived at injustices committed by reactionary
powers. His error was perhaps one of omission. Philip Thody
has pointed out that *L'Homme Révolté* makes no mention of
the 'limited' revolt displayed by both the British Labour Party
and the American trade-union movement, both of which had
avoided the passage to totalitarianism and should deserve
credit in Camus's account.[2] The same author has counted
the number of writers referred to in the pages of *L'Homme
Révolté* (one hundred and sixty) and the number of historical
characters (ninety-six) and concludes, I think correctly, that
the treatment of them is over-simplified.

L'Homme Révolté does not appeal to a reader with the

---

[1] p. 19. 'There are means which cannot be excused.'
[2] Philip Thody, op. cit., p. 140.

intellectual rigour of Jean-Paul Sartre because it is less a study than an autobiography. In an interview in *Gazette des Lettres* (15 February 1952), Camus said that his book was a 'personal experience . . . a confidence'.[1] It is the account of the journey of a mind through history, undertaken in an attempt to solve the intolerable riddle that men were more good than bad, yet committed more evil acts than good ones. Because Camus was such a sensitive man, he found the attempt painful, and could only solve it with a compromise.

* * *

Politics and Journalism

In the light of the above comments on *L'Homme Révolté* and the subsequent controversy with Sartre, we can turn to the vast body of political writings, some of which Camus assembled under the collective title *Actuelles*, and see how he applied his principles to specific issues. The first thing we notice is that these articles are written with much more care than is customary in day to day journalism, and secondly that Camus was steadfast and consistent in his adherence to the spirit of moderation.

Camus maintained that journalism should be both truthful and critical. He advocated the printing of conflicting views on the same page and a clear statement as to the source of news which might be controversial. A newspaper should be free to print the truth, whatever it may be, and free to make objective, independent, and intelligent comment. The journalist was duty-bound to interpret the news in a way which would make its implications and consequences clear. He must avoid clichés, resist propaganda, expose abuses, and above all ruthlessly draw attention to humbug.

Dr Cruickshank has noted that Camus's concern for moderation in journalism and politics brought him much closer to the English political tradition than to the doctrinaire, uncompromising approach typical of the French.[2] He was deter-

[1] Bibliothèque de la Pléiade, *Essais*, p. 743.
[2] John Cruickshank, op. cit., p. 131.

mined to avoid extremism at all times, which accounts for his final inability to please anyone; it is noteworthy that *L'Homme Révolté* provoked attacks from the Right just as virulent as those which came from the Left. On the whole, he distrusted politicians who used words to which he attached importance, and devalued, degraded and cheapened them with dishonourable motives. 'Chaque fois que j'entends un discours politique', he wrote, 'je suis effrayé depuis des années de n'entendre rien qui rende un son humain. Ce sont toujours les mêmes mots qui disent les mêmes mensonges.'[1] Camus hoped to restore honour to politics ('une politique de l'honneur', as he said in *Lettres à un Ami Allemand*), an intention which he saw lamentably debased by those who paid lip-service to it. In the name of French honour, he wrote, the Right has too often perpetrated that which was the most contrary to honour.[2] A stern moralist, he wanted to see political life based on solid foundations of honesty and respect for the truth.

Apart from his brief spell with the Communist party in his youth, Camus did not belong to a political party. But he was most in sympathy with those Socialist parties which approached closest to a democratic ideal. He firmly believed that the democratic processes were workable, a belief which is in line with his principle of *la mesure*. When all is said and done, he said, a democrat is someone who admits that his adversary might be right, is prepared to listen to him, and to reflect on what he says.[3] In an article in *Caliban*, November 1948, he wrote a definition of democracy which is fairly familiar – democracy is not the best of régimes: it is simply the least bad. The democrat is modest. He recognizes that he does not know everything, and must consult others who can complement his knowledge. He recognizes also that he is no more than a representative, and that whatever decisions he may make can

---

[1] *Carnets*, p. 64. 'For years now, every time I hear a political speech, I am frightened because I hear nothing which sounds human. They are always the same words telling the same lies.' (BM)

[2] *Actuelles* III, p. 19.

[3] *Actuelles* I, p. 125.

be revoked by those who have placed him in this position and whose collective judgement is contrary to his own. He is aware that the majority might be wrong, when the minority is right, and that is why he says democracy is not the best of systems. But on balance it is better to put up with a certain sluggishness than to sacrifice all to speed. The minority will, with some delay, be heard, and account will be taken of its views.

In spite of the fact that he had belonged to the Communist Party in 1935, had taken his first journalistic assignment with a left-wing paper, *L'Alger Républicain*, and for most of his life been identified with left-wing views, Camus grew more and more disenchanted with Russian communism, and eventually became known as an anti-Communist writer. He detested the opportunism of communism, and its ruthless subordination of all principles, including its own, to the eventual establishment of a glorious Utopia. In *L'Homme Révolté* he compared communism with fascism:

> Il n'est pas juste d'identifier les fins du fascisme et du communisme russe. Le premier figure l'exaltation du bourreau par le bourreau lui-même. Le second, plus dramatique, l'exaltation du bourreau par les victimes. Le premier n'a jamais rêvé de libérer tout l'homme, mais seulement d'en libérer quelques-uns en subjuguant les autres. Le second, dans son principe le plus profond, vise à libérer tous les hommes en les asservissant tous, provisoirement.[1]

Fascism and communism are equally the products of moral nihilism, he says. More pertinently, communism is rotten in conception ('dans son principe le plus profond'), a view with which Sartre violently disagreed, holding that the principles of communism had often been betrayed by bad communists, but

[1] *L'Homme Révolté*, p. 293. 'It is not legitimate to identify the ends of Fascism with the ends of Russian communism. The first represents the exaltation of the executioner by the executioner; the second, more dramatic in concept, the exaltation of the executioner by the victim. The former never dreamed of liberating all men, but only of liberating a few by subjugating the rest. The latter, in its most profound principle, aims at liberating all men by provisionally enslaving them all.'

that the ideal itself was inviolate. It is awesome to recall that it was Camus whom the Communist Party newspaper *L'Humanité* called the 'writer of illusion'.

There is, however, little truth in the charge, already mentioned, that Camus only denounced violence on the Left. A careful reading of his articles shows that he opposed force from whatever quarter it came and exposed intolerance under whatever name it was cloaked. He maintained a resolute impartiality which made him enemies on both sides. You cannot decide whether an idea is right or wrong according to whether it comes from the right or from the left, he wrote, still less according to what the right or left elect to do with it.[1] Camus's admirers could not forgive him for sitting on the fence and refusing to jump one way or the other. Instead of distinguishing between 'right' and 'left', he distinguished between 'brutes' and 'victims', and found evidence of each in both camps. (A whole series of articles in *Actuelles I* is known collectively as *Ni bourreaux, ni victimes*.) His severe moral honesty prompted him to point the finger at thugs whatever their political persuasion. A brief glance at some of the issues on which he spoke out testifies to his impartiality. He was uncompromisingly opposed to the brutal dictatorship of Franco, resigning from UNESCO in 1952 as a protest against the admission of Spain. The following year, he defended the cause of the workers and their spontaneous uprising in East Berlin and denounced their fearsome suppression by the Russian army. 'When a worker shakes his naked fist at a tank and cries that he is not a slave, what are we if we remain indifferent?' he said in a speech at the time.[2] In 1947 he had spoken out against the repression of a revolt in Madagascar by the colonial French forces, and in 1956 against the repression of the Hungarian uprising by the colonial Russian forces.[3] In 1948 he defended Greek communists who had been sentenced to death. He constantly opposed legalized murder under the

---

[1] *Actuelles* I, p. 86.
[2] *Pléiade*, p. xxxvi.
[3] Pléiade, *Essais*, p. 322.

guise of capital punishment, pointing out that it was not only disgusting and abhorrent, but inefficient (since it did not deter) and unhealthy, since the number of applications for post of hangman always far outnumbered the positions available. In 1957, Camus's *Réflexions sur la Guillotine* appeared in an edition with Koestler's *Reflexions on Hanging*. As any reader of *L'Etranger* and *La Peste* will know, Camus loathed executioners, whether they were Spanish, Russian, French, or German.

Camus had the ability, usually lacking in politicians and their friends, to feel and share the misery of vast numbers of people. He suffered at the thought that millions had been killed in the name of liberty. That this quality was perceived by the ordinary man, over the heads of political reviewers, is testified by the anonymous postcard he received from Barcelona (besieged by Franco's Fascist Army), on which was written the simple word 'Gracias'. Already in 1939, his articles in *L'Alger-Republicain* describing the plight of the Kabyl people in the throes of famine indicated that the primary emotion which impelled Camus into political journalism was compassion. The compassion was not selective; Camus was utterly devoid of racial discrimination, an evil which he denounced in countless articles (see, for instance, *Combat*, 10 May 1947). Nevertheless he was accused, and is still accused, of harbouring an inbred prejudice against the Arabs of his native Algeria.

The Algerian war of independence, which began in 1954, was a particularly acute personal tragedy for Albert Camus. As an Algerian of European stock, whose cultural home was Paris, he naturally saw the problem from the inside. It was exacerbated by his refusal to think in terms of black and white. We have seen that, long before the war started, he was awaking attention to the plight of the Kabyls. Profoundly conscious of the evils of colonialism and the suffering of oppressed peoples, he was in the forefront in defending the rights of the Arabs, to whom, he said, reparation must be made. But, with customary impartiality, he would not forget the rights of the French population who were just as 'native' to Algeria as the Arabs, and who could not be sacrificed to fashionable political expediency. He advocated the continuance of the French connection in Algeria on the grounds that the country could not survive without economic support from France. It is more than likely that strong emotional grounds also played a part. (He could not bear the thought that he might one day need a passport to enter his native land. *Pléiade*, p. 1844.) He came close to supporting actual French rule, and while he denounced extremists on both sides, the fact remains that his comments on the repressive actions of the French were less frequent than his unequivocal denunciation of the Algerian nationalists. The impression gained ground that he was lukewarm in his comments on French repression, and the impression has persisted. Those interested in forming their own opinion should read the many articles on the subject reprinted in the *Pléiade* edition (for example, the articles of 9 July and 23 July 1955, in *L'Express*, pp. 1865 et seq.), in which Camus was adamant in his condemnation of torture 'whether in Budapest or Algeria', and also the letter to *Encounter* dated June 1957. Camus also personally intervened with Presidents Coty and de Gaulle on many occasions to plead clemency for condemned Arab terrorists, without publicity; a list of some of the men he defended in this way is to be found in *Pléiade*, pp. 1845–6. He said that terrorism and blind suppression were equally destructive, yet the feeling spread that Camus was, for once, on the wrong side. It was not enough that he should demand economic equality for the Arabs, when what they wanted was the freedom to decide their own future and choose their own friends. Camus was appealing for a change of heart in the colonial power, while avoiding the conclusion that the colonial power should pay for its years of exploitation by leaving Algeria altogether. On 22 January 1956, Camus made a well-publicized appeal, in Algiers, for a truce; he asked that the FLN (Algerian nationalists) and the French army should both declare that they would not violate the rights, freedom, and safety of the civilian population. It was an appeal for moderation in accordance with the precepts of *L'Homme Révolté*. To the Arabs it seemed like an invitation to acquiesce in their state of oppression and to co-operate in maintaining the *status quo:* to the French, it seemed like a betrayal of his own people. Camus's plea had no effect whatever, and he returned to Paris dejected and despondent. His friends say he was broken-hearted. From that time, he scarcely uttered a word on the Algerian problem, and died before it was resolved. He might not have been happy with the eventual solution.

Camus's recommendations were derived from his own generosity of spirit. But in an extreme situation, where they had to be put to the test, they were found to be useless. One cannot disagree with a man who says that it is wrong to kill people, that the rights of the individual must be respected, that moderation is a virtue. But having agreed, how far has one advanced? Pained by a problem which hurt him on every level of his being, Camus withdrew into generalities which were too universal to be of immediate value. People grew bored, and stopped listening.

6

La Chute

Apart from a collection of essays written between 1939 and 1953 (*L'Eté*), and two theatrical adaptations, Camus's literary work lay in abeyance for some years. Then he astonished his public in 1956 by publishing a novel which was so totally different in spirit from all his previous work that many people were to suppose it reflected a serious crisis in his moral life. We know that he was depressed by the row over *L'Homme Révolté*, and by the disaster of Algeria. While it would be quite wrong to assume that *La Chute* offers a self-portrait, it does certainly give an indication of a state of mind. A happier man could not have written this book.

The narrator is Jean-Baptiste Clamence. He is in a seedy waterfront bar in Amsterdam and he is talking to another man whom he has pigeon-holed, and whose comments we only learn by inference from Clamence's own words. The entire book is within quotation marks, a long, witty, articulate and cynical monologue, a self-indulgent confession of guilt. It appears that Clamence used to be a happy man. He was a successful Parisian lawyer, highly respected, liked and admired. A man of generosity and warmth, he made a habit of offering his services free of charge to the poor. He would always comfort and assuage the afflicted. He was devoted to charitable causes. Clamence was well-known in Paris, in fact, as a good man who used his extraordinary gift of eloquence in the service of his fellows. He enjoyed the simple pleasures of life, did not bask in his popularity, was modest and unselfish. Then, one evening as he was crossing a bridge over the Seine, he had a terrible experience. A young woman committed suicide by throwing herself into the river. He heard the splash and her cries for help, but he did not turn back, he did not even look to see if she could be helped. He pretended that it had never happened (he wished it had not), walked on, and abandoned the woman to her death. The memory of that moment of cowardice has lived with him ever since, and has ruined him. He now sees himself as a fraud, an imposter. He examines himself minutely, and finds nothing but mediocrity, lies, deceit. Every item of his past life is reinterpreted in the light of this experience, and found to be hypocritical. He was a sham, a fake, an egotist who disguised his self-absorption even from himself. He now realizes that his good deeds were always done before an audience, that they ceased whenever there was no one to applaud them. Haunted with remorse, Clamence took refuge for a while in debauchery, then gave up his law practice and came to Amsterdam, where we now meet him, a sardonic, bitter man, full of self-loathing. He collars unsuspecting victims in bars, subjects them to a confession, then subtly makes them realize that he is describing not one man, but all men, and by implication his present victim, whose self-esteem he slowly breaks so that, at the end of the day, the victim has seen himself in the mirror held up by Clamence, and assumes his burden of shame. Clamence now uses his mastery of language not for the salvation of others, but for their destruction.

La Chute is a distressing book, and I am sure it was distressing to write. The mirror is held up to the reader as well as to Clamence's immediate victim. It is an embarrassingly accurate account of pharisaism, a probing, surgical, merciless revelation of that part of hypocrisy in us all which, when we admit it in times of introspection, causes us our most despairing moments.

We are a long way from the joy for living which has so far characterized all Camus's work. Clamence is the very anti-thesis of Sisyphus, or Dr Rieux, or Rambert, because he has given in to selfishness and despair. Indeed, he seems at times hardly to have been created from the same pen. Rieux said that men were fundamentally more good than bad; Clamence says that they are uniformly despicable in their very essence. Where *La Chute* bears a relation to Camus's other work is in its obsession with the theme of lost innocence. Meursault had primal innocence. Tarrou and Kaliayev both strove to remain innocent in an evil world; Clamence shows that their endeavour is impossible, for evil is within us.

We must become a little better acquainted with Clamence before deciding what were Camus's intentions in creating such a destructive man. First of all, he is fluent and articulate, never at a loss for words. With beguiling self-mockery he says, 'dès que j'ouvre la bouche, les phrases coulent'.[1] An unremitting battery of words is the first weapon he uses to cow his victim.

His second weapon is honesty. He seeks to gain the listener's confidence by laying bare his own hypocrisy and thus anticipating any accusation which might be levelled against him. '. . . je gagnais ma vie en dialoguant avec des gens que je méprisais',[2] he says. He claims to recognize that, as a lawyer, he made use of modesty in order to shine, of humility in order to conquer, and of virtue in order to oppress. He trumpeted his loyalty to friends, and there was not one of them whom he did not finally betray. If he helped his neighbour, it was only to indulge the pleasure he personally derived therefrom. 'Toujours est-il qu'après de longues études sur moi-même, j'ai mis au jour la duplicité profonde de la créature.'[3] From introspective honesty about himself, Clamence almost imperceptibly moves to a position of accuser. He infers that duplicity is common to all men, and warns the listener not to trust those of his friends who ask him to be sincere in his evaluation of them: 'Ils espèrent seulement que vous les entretiendrez dans la bonne idée qu'ils ont d'eux-mêmes, en les fournissant d'une certitude supplémentaire qu'ils puiseront dans votre promesse de sincérité. . . . Si, donc, vous vous trouvez dans ce cas,

[1] p. 8. 'As soon as I open my mouth, sentences pour out.'

[2] p. 11. 'I earned my living by dealing with people whom I despised.' (BM)

[3] p. 47. 'However that may be, after prolonged research on myself, I brought out the basic duplicity of the human being.'

n'hésitez pas: promettez d'être vrai et mentez le mieux possible. Vous répondrez à leur désir profond et leur prouverez doublement votre affection.'[1] Having implied that hypocrisy is a natural condition of humanity, Clamence switches his accusation from the general to the particular and entraps his victim with the reflection that we only confide in those who resemble us and who share our weaknesses. By confiding in the listener, he implies that he has recognized a fellow-hypocrite.

Clamence's incurable introspection derives in the first instance from vanity. He has examined his own motives because he is fascinated by himself, and has contrived to make other people fascinated too. He always wanted to be seen and admired by the greatest possible number, and generally succeeded (p. 15). Surely he was perfectly normal to behave so? Only he admits his vanity, where others deny it. 'Il faut le reconnaître humblement, mon cher compatriote, j'ai toujours crevé de vanité. Moi, moi, moi, voilà le refrain de ma chère vie, et qui s'entendait dans tout ce que je disais.'[2] He further concedes that he has never loved anyone as much as himself and goes on to confess another painful truth, that we only love in others the image of ourselves which we see thrown back at us and that to render this comforting image permanent, we should rather see the loved one dead than watch the love die: 'Dans mes moments d'agacement, je me disais alors que la solution idéale eût été la mort pour la personne qui m'intéressait. Cette mort eût définitivement fixé notre lien . . .'[3] In other words, Clamence admits that love has only been useful to him in so far as it has flattered his narcissism. In this con-

---

[1] p. 46. 'They merely hope you will encourage them in the good opinion they have of themselves by providing them with the additional assurance they find in your promise of sincerity. . . . Therefore, if you are in that situation, don't hesitate: promise to tell the truth and lie as best you can. You will satisfy their hidden desire and doubly prove your affection.'

[2] p. 27. 'I have to admit it humbly, *mon cher compatriote*, I was always bursting with vanity. I, I, I is the refrain of my whole life and it could be heard in everything I said.'

[3] p. 37. 'In my moments of irritation I told myself that the ideal solution would have been the death of the person I was interested in. Her death would have fixed our relationship once and for all.'

nection, it is interesting to see how Camus has constructed his book so that the listener is denied any independent existence and functions only as a receptacle for Clamence's egoism. The self-vilification of his technique masks a perverse self-glorification; the important element is that the attention should be directed towards himself. There is a large degree of sado-masochism in his behaviour. Clamence invites the listener to despise him, then delights in his discomfiture when he realizes that his contempt may be directed towards his own behaviour, since it is no better than Clamence's. So absolute is this vanity, that Clamence invites the listener to admire the technique of his speech. He says that he adapts it according to whom he is with, that he has more or less learnt by heart what he has to say, but is able to improvise if necessary. This is the vanity of an actor, who plays with his audience as a cat does with a mouse, manipulates their emotions, and then looks to be praised by them for doing it well.

The arrogance and pride of morbid egoism are shown in the bland self-satisfaction which Clamence feels at having climbed to a summit of self-knowledge from which he can judge others and contemplate their absurd, deceitful pantomime. Yet there is something pathetic in this parade of self-esteem. One suspects that Clamence is no longer a happy individual, despite his protestations to the contrary (p. 79), and would dearly love to reconstruct the pieces of his shattered personality. Secretly, he is calling for help.

For the moment, however, Clamence glories in cynicism. A selection of his remarks reveals the depth of disillusion from which he suffers, and also the swingeing accuracy of his observation. He notes that people enjoy, selfishly, the spectacle of tragedy and drama in their friends' lives because it gives them an opportunity to display their grief, to show their emotion, tacitly to vaunt themselves (p. 19). He says that the motto of his house is 'Don't place your trust here' (p. 26). There are people who make it a profession to pardon all faults, forgive all offence; but these are the very people who never forget (p. 28). For some, the most difficult thing in the world is to resist taking possession of a person whom one does not really want (p. 35). On suicide, Clamence says that you must not expect your gesture to be interpreted in the way you intended that it should; people do not imagine that you may kill yourself for two reasons, not one; and they will vulgarize and diminish your act after your death: 'Vous mort, ils en profiteront pour donner à votre geste des motifs idiots, ou vulgaires. Les martyrs, cher ami, doivent choisir d'être oubliés, raillés ou utilisés. Quant à être compris, jamais.'[1] Don't believe people who beg you to be sincere with them; tell them a few lies, and they will be happy (p. 46). Debauchery and promiscuity suit a narcissist because they create no obligations (p. 57). We must forgive the Pope, firstly because he needs forgiveness more than anyone, secondly because it is the only way to gain ascendancy over him (p. 70). There is always an explanation for murder, never for letting somebody live (p. 62). Most of the time, Clamence employs cynicism in this way as a means to shock and paralyse his listener. But at the very end of his confession comes the most cynical and truthful admission of all, when one sees that this is a method of self-protection. If he could live his experience all over again, if the young woman would once more throw herself into the river, if he had the chance to retrieve himself, would he take it? No, says Clamence. He knows very well that he would do the same again, he would be a coward again and walk on the other side. Because he is human and that is what human beings do. It is useless to pretend that we can change.

We have seen that Clamence's pitiless self-indictment hides a multitude of ulterior motives. In spite of appearances, he lacks self-confidence, hastens to parade his insufficiencies before anyone else discovers them, treats them with a wry shrug of the shoulders and a percipient irony which makes a semi-joke of them. These are the methods of a man who has

[1] p. 42. 'Once you are dead, they will take advantage of it to attribute idiotic or vulgar motives to your action. Martyrs, *cher ami*, must choose between being forgotten, mocked, or made use of. As for being understood – never!'

abdicated to despair. There is nothing for him to do but grow older, which alone requires a superhuman effort. He says, 'Oui, on peut faire la guerre en ce monde, singer l'amour, torturer son semblable, parader dans les journaux, ou simplement dire du mal de son voisin en tricotant. Mais, dans certains cas, continuer, seulement continuer, voilà ce qui est surhumain.'[1]

The cause of this despair is not far to seek. *La Chute* of the title is the fall from a state of innocence, which, in Clamence's case, can be located specifically in time to the dreadful night on the bridge. That moment opened the door to Clamence's rigorous psycho-analytic self-examination from which ordeal he has not yet emerged. The exercise has convinced him that all his actions have been dictated by self-interest, and he is stained with guilt, irremediably and perpetually. 'L'idée la plus naturelle à l'homme, celle qui lui vient naïvement, comme du fond de sa nature, est l'idée de son innocence.'[2] It is Clamence's tragedy to have found that this assumption of innocence is false; he has carried even further Tarrou's intimation of an 'interior plague' and declares that the disease which makes man commit evil is incurable. 'Nous pouvons affirmer à coup sûr la culpabilité de tous.'[3] 'Il fallait se soumettre et reconnaître sa culpabilité. Il fallait vivre dans le malconfort.'[4] With this frightening knowledge Clamence must confess. He has no God, so he must confess to men, he must make himself a penitent. At the same time, to alleviate this overwhelming sense of guilt, he must pass on some of the burden to others, so he must be judge as well. 'Il faut s'accabler soi-même pour avoir le droit de

---

[1] p. 63. 'Yes, you can make war in this world, you can go through the motions of love-making, you can torture your fellow man, you can prostitute yourself in the newspapers, or you can simply say nasty things about your neighbour, while knitting. But in certain cases, to go on, simply to go on, is superhuman.' (BM)

[2] p. 44. 'The idea that comes most naturally to man, most naïvely, as if from his very nature, is the idea of his innocence.'

[3] p. 61. 'We can state with certainty the guilt of all.'

[4] p. 60. 'I had to submit and admit my guilt. I had to live in the little-ease.' ('discomfort' – BM)

juger les autres.'[1] He calls himself a 'judge-penitent', at once accuser and defendant, and he maintains that such is the basis of social intercourse; the relationship between men and men hinges on the distribution of guilt – they are all accusers and defendants. For his part, he will be a merciless judge, the better to avoid being placed in the position of defendant. 'Pas d'excuses, jamais, pour personne, voilà mon principe, au départ. Je nie la bonne intention, l'erreur estimable, le faux pas, la circonstance atténuante. Chez moi, on ne bénit pas, on ne distribue pas d'absolution. On fait l'addition, simplement . . .'[2] The accusers dominate, the penitents cower, and such is the state of affairs proper to the human condition.

There is something intolerably solitary in such dark pessimism as this. One can imagine Clamence wandering from bar to bar, night after night, seducing strangers with his eloquence and insidious penetration, emerging victorious, and resuming his solitude when the battle is won. Meursault was a 'stranger' to human society because he was fundamentally innocent; Clamence feels himself a stranger because he is steeped in guilt, and the only method he has to relieve his unbearable isolation is to convince others of their guilt so that he is no longer an alien among them, but resembles them like a brother. His greatest error, however, is to think in terms of absolutes. He is surely wrong to say that a moment of cowardice had branded him with guilt everlasting, just as he is wrong to say that he was totally innocent before that event. As for his re-interpretation of his past in the light of this event, he is again wrong to depict it as uniformly hypocritical. Human behaviour is always subject to diverse interpretations, and every human act may be seen as 'good' or 'bad', 'honest' or 'deceitful', 'selfish' or 'unselfish' according to the way in which it is approached. It may deserve all of these adjectives at the same

---

[1] p. 76. 'One had to overwhelm oneself to have the right to judge others.'

[2] p. 72. 'No excuses ever, for anyone; that's my principle at the outset. I deny the good intention, the respectable mistake, the indiscretion, the extenuating circumstance. With me there is no giving of absolution or blessing. Everything is simply totted up.'

time. There is an essential ambiguity in the motives of human actions of which Clamence does not take account. There is a measure of hypocrisy in us all, and a measure of self-interest; there is always a measure of genuinely disinterested altruism, and a measure of sincerity. Clamence assumes that because he is not absolutely innocent he must be absolutely guilty. He is wrong in both assumptions.

The obsession with universal guilt has led more than a few commentators to make the obvious parallel with some items of Christian dogma. It was suggested that Camus was moving towards conversion. *La Chute* was a fall from the state of grace and Clamence's previous innocence was his Eden. His name is an echo of John the Baptist, and the surname suggests the *vox clamantis in deserto*; John baptised in water, Clamence's fall was precipitated by a tragedy in water. The canals of Amsterdam are carefully compared with the circles of Dante's Hell. Yet more fanciful parallels can be drawn. Camus specifically rejected the Christian interpretation which had been imposed on his book in an interview in *Le Monde* in 1956. Nothing really justifies such a view, he said. He admired the life and death of the first Christian, but 'mon manque d'imagination m'interdit de le suivre plus loin'.[1] He further insisted that this was the only point of similarity between Clamence and his creator.

It seems incredible that anyone should imagine *La Chute* was a portrait of the author. Clamence negates every principle which Camus proclaimed. His cynical view of life is the very antithesis of Camus's obstinate optimism and a betrayal of that faith in man which animated all his previous works. No, this is not a portrait of Camus, but a portrait of his detractors, those who had told him that his mild liberalism and naive faith were lacking in vigour. Sartre had accused him of being an alms-giver; with gentle irony, Clamence refers to his charitable deeds before his fall and admits that he enjoyed being an almoner. When Clamence claims to represent Everyman ('je fabrique un portrait qui est celui de tous et de personne . . .

[1] 'My lack of imagination prevents me from following him any further.'

le portrait que je tends à mes contemporains devient un miroir'[1]),
he is not echoing Camus, but those of his contemporaries who
were afflicted with sterile cynicism and thought that men had
to be led by the nose towards Utopia because, left to their own
devices, they would squabble in a standing position. If *La
Chute* is a satire, it is a satire on communist philosophy. Camus
loved men even in their failings.

Furthermore, I do not think it has been sufficiently noticed
that *La Chute* is a protest against the misuse of language.
Throughout his career, Camus was consistent in his demand that
language should serve as an instrument of clarification. Every
one of his books bears the mark of this preoccupation in some
way, and the majority of his articles touch upon it. Meursault
in *L'Etranger* used language as a simple means of direct and
honest communication; he had not learnt its power to dis-
semble. In *La Peste*, Rieux and Tarrou make frequent allusion
to the necessity of facing facts by means of language which is
clear, truthful and unequivocal; Grand excites pity because he
is unable to express himself; Paneloux is castigated for concealing the truth beneath a cloak of obfuscating rhetoric
which confuses rather than elucidates. The play *Le Malentendu*
presents a tragedy which need not have occurred had Jan told
the truth in the first place and revealed his identity. In his
political articles, Camus reproaches politicians for wilfully
eluding the truth in language which is designed to deceive.
La Chute offers us a picture of the ultimate degradation of
language employed to enslave and reduce the listener. For
Camus, communication between men was the means by which
they recognized each other and asserted their solidarity in the
fight against an unjust world, and he could not bring himself to
forgive men who used words to diminish or distort the human
experience.

La Chute is the result of Camus's dogged refusal to succomb
to the temptations of pessimism. That the temptations were
there is made manifest by the force of the bitter ironical tone

[1] 'I paint a portrait of everyone and of no one in particular . . . the picture
which I show my contemporaries becomes a mirror.' (BM)

in which the book is written. Camus's remedy against this 'inner plague' was to isolate it and write about it. The monologue is set in a scene alien to him – the dank, misty darkness of Amsterdam, contrasting so forcefully with the sunny, warm, life-enhancing atmosphere of North Africa, where *L'Etranger* and *La Peste* are set. The insidious fine rain of Amsterdam which seeps through the skin corresponds to the malignant poisonous cynicism which possesses Clamence. Camus died before he was able to write another sunny book.

*   *   *

In 1957 Camus published a slim volume of short stories under the title *L'Exil et le Royaume*, and on 17 October of that year, he discarded his habitual belted raincoat and donned white tie and tails to receive the Nobel Prize for Literature in Stockholm. He adapted two more plays, including Faulkner's *Requiem for a Nun*. (In answer to further suppositions of imminent conversion, he said, 'if I had translated and produced a Greek tragedy, no one would have asked me if I believed in Zeus'.) Two years later, he adapted Dostoievsky's *The Possessed*. He was also working on a novel to be called *Le Premier Homme*. On 5 January 1960, he was travelling to Paris in a fast car driven by Michel Gallimard. The car unaccountably skidded and drove into a tree. Albert Camus died instantly. He was forty-six years old.

Bibliography

A. An indispensable book of reference for students is the complete works of Albert Camus published in two volumes by Gallimard in the *Bibliothèque de la Pléiade*. It contains valuable commentaries by M. Roger Quilliot, a history of the conception of each book based on Camus's notes and manuscript sources, a selection of additional articles and reviews, some private letters, and an exhaustive bibliography of Camus's journalism.

B. EDITIONS OF CAMUS'S WORKS USED IN THE PRESENT STUDY
La Mort Heureuse, edited by Jean Sarocchi, Gallimard, 1971.
L'Envers et L'Endroit, 'Collection Idées', Gallimard, 1958.
Noces, 'Collection Folio', Gallimard, 1959.
L'Etranger, edited by Germaine Brée and Carlos Lynnes, Methuen Educational, 1958.
Le Mythe de Sisyphe, 'Collection Idées', Gallimard, 1942.
La Peste, edited by W. J. Strachan, Methuen Educational, 1959.
Lettres à un Ami Allemand, Gallimard, 1948.
Le Malentendu and *Caligula*, Gallimard, 1958.
L'Homme Révolté, 'Collection Idées', Gallimard, 1951.
L'Etat de Siège, Gallimard, 1948.
Les Justes, edited by Edward O. Marsh, Harrap, 1960.
L'Eté, 'Collection Folio', Gallimard, 1959 (same volume as *Noces*).
La Chute, edited by B. G. Garnham. Methuen Educational, 1971.
L'Exil et le Royaume, 'Collection Folio', Gallimard, 1957.
Actuelles I, Gallimard, 1950.
Actuelles II, Gallimard, 1953.
Actuelles III (*Chroniques Algériennes*), Gallimard, 1958.
Réflexions sur la Guillotine, Calmann-Lévy, 1957.
Discours de Suède, Gallimard, 1958.

C. TRANSLATIONS USED IN FOOTNOTE FOR THE PRESENT STUDY
The Outsider, translated by Stuart Gilbert (Hamish Hamilton, 1946).

The Myth of Sisyphus, translated by Justin O'Brien (Hamish Hamilton, 1955).

The Plague, translated by Stuart Gilbert (Hamish Hamilton, 1959).

The Rebel, translated by Anthony Bower (Hamish Hamilton, 1959).

The Fall, translated by Justin O'Brien (Hamish Hamilton, 1957).

The Just Assassins, translated by Stuart Gilbert (Knopf, New York, 1962).

Lyrical and Critical (contains *Betwixt and Between*, *Nuptials*, *Summer*, critical essays and some interviews), translated by Philip Thody (Hamish Hamilton, 1967).

Resistance, Rebellion and Death (contains *Letters to a German Friend*, Camus's address to the Dominican Friars, and political articles), translated by Justin O'Brien (Hamish Hamilton, 1961).

D. A SELECTION OF BOOKS ON CAMUS

Brée, Germaine, *Camus*, Rutgers University Press, 1959.

Brisville, Jean-Claude, *Camus*, 'La Bibliothèque Idéale', Gallimard, 1960.

Champigny, Robert, *Sur un héros paien*, 'Les Essais', Gallimard, 1959.

Costes, Alain, *Albert Camus on La Parole Manquante*, Payot, 1973.

Cruickshank, John, *Albert Camus and the Literature of Revolt*, Oxford University Press, 1959.

Ginestier, Paul, *La Pensée de Camus*, Bordas, 1964.

Haggis, D. R., *La Peste*, 'Studies in French Literature', Edward Arnold, 1962.

King, Adèle, *Camus*, 'Writers and Critics', Oliver & Boyd, 1964.

Luppé, Robert de, *Albert Camus*, 'Classiques du XXᵉ Siècle', Editions Universitaires, 1952.

O'Brien, Conor Cruise, *Camus*, 'Modern Masters', Fontana, 1970.

Onimus, Jean, *Camus*, 'Les écrivains devant Dieu', Desclée de Brouwer, 1965.

Rey, Pierre-Louis, *La Chute*, 'Profil d'une Œuvre', Hatier, 1970.

Sarocchi, Jean, *Camus*, Presses Universitaires de France, 1968.

Scott, Nathan A., *Albert Camus*, Bowes & Bowes, 1962.

Thody, Philip, *Albert Camus 1913–1960*, Hamish Hamilton, 1961.

Quilliot, Roger, *La Mer et les Prisons*, Gallimard, 1956.

E. ARTICLES ON CAMUS

The list of occasional articles, in books and in periodicals, is enormous. Students are referred to bibliographies in books by Cruickshank, Thody, and Brisville, mentioned above, and also

Calepins de Bibliographie published in Minard (1968). Of special interest are the two issues of *Les Temps Modernes* for May and August 1952, in which students will find the discussion of *L'Homme Révolté* by Jeanson, Sartre and Camus, and also Sartre's critical review of *L'Etranger* in *Situations I,* Gallimard, 1947.